New Religious Move:
Series Editor: Peter

THE WAY OF THE HEART

The Rajneesh Movement

THE WAY OF THE HEART

The Rajneesh Movement

by

Judith Thompson and Paul Heelas

Department of Religious Studies, University of Lancaster

THE AQUARIAN PRESS
Wellingborough, Northamptonshire

First published 1986

British Library Cataloguing in Publication Data

Thompson, Judith
    The way of the heart: the Rajneesh movement
    — (New religious movement series)
    1. Rajneesh Foundation International
    I. Title   II. Heelas, Paul   III. Series
    294.5   BP605.R342

ISBN 0-85030-434-2

*The Aquarian Press is part of the
Thorsons Publishing Group*

Printed and bound in Great Britain

Contents

Acknowledgement

We wish to thank all those sannyasins who did so much to help us to understand their path. In particular, thanks goes to those who were prepared to let us include their words and to those who contributed photographs. We would also like to acknowledge friends who have assisted us during our work, especially Anne-Marie, Paul, Nandana and Karen. Lastly thanks to Michael Cox for his patience and good humour and to Peter Clarke who provided the initial impetus for this book.

Judith Thompson and Paul Heelas.

Series Editor's Preface

New religions abound in contemporary Britain. As many as five hundred have been established since 1945. These religious derive from many different cultures and have given rise to much controversy in the media and in every walk of life — politics, medicine, education, the law, and the churches.

The methods of recruitment, aims, purposes, rituals, and practices of a number of these movements have all been hotly debated and observers have been led to ask to what extent, if any, some of these movements may reasonably be regarded as religious and enjoy the benefits, for example, of charitable status. On the other hand, there are those who see them as a clear indication of 'the return of the sacred' to modern society, which it was widely assumed was undergoing an inexorable process of secularization.

One thing is clear to those involved in the field of new religions: it is impossible to generalize about them. While a number do hold similar beliefs and pursue similar goals, new religions come in all shapes and sizes and are often very different from one another. That is why it is important to consider each of these religions separately before attempting to reach any overall conclusions concerning the phenomenon of new religions, and this also explains in large measure the purpose of this series.

In each book an attempt will be made to provide an objective account of a particular movement, its origins, development, beliefs, practices, aims, and appeal, and the response to it of the wider society. Some of the controversial issues surrounding these movements will also be discussed and the authors have been given the freedom to express their own opinion, based on the evidence available to them, on these matters. Technical language has been avoided wherever possible with the intention of making the series available to the widest possible readership.

PETER B. CLARKE
King's College, London

Introduction

Bhagwan Shree Rajneesh is in the news. Leader of a large religious movement, frequently referred to as the 'Orange People', he has recently been found guilty of criminal offences. For someone who claims to be God, this is perhaps extraordinary. Indeed, Bhagwan's whole career as a spiritual Master has been extraordinary. He has broken convention after convention. The ashram which he ran in India during the 1970s was the scene of outrageous behaviour. Many felt that the sexual and emotional excesses that took place in the ashram are hardly compatible with Bhagwan's claim to be enlightened. More recently, the ashram he ran in America was the scene of conspicuous consumption. Ninety-three Rolls Royces, five hundred other cars, one hundred air conditioned buses, and five aeroplanes: hardly the mark of someone who teaches the eastern path of detachment.

It is hard for us in the west to take Bhagwan seriously. Most accounts have taken the form of 'exposés'. Journalists, film makers, and academics have poked fun at Bhagwan. There is also a strong tendency for them to dismiss him as a charlatan, a fraud, or a capitalist. In this book we adopt a different approach. As anthropologists, our main aim is to convey the nature of Bhagwan's teaching and the life of his followers, the sannyasins. We feel that it is important to make as much sense of Bhagwan's path as possible before moving on to adopt a more critical perspective. Accordingly, it is only in the last chapter or so that we place the Neo-Sannyas International Movement (to give it its proper name) under scrutiny.

Our 'making sense of' approach reflects our opinion that Bhagwan's path is worthy of consideration in its own right. Far from being a deviant movement, Bhagwan's path exemplifies some of the more interesting developments in contemporary culture. We are thinking of those developments to do with psycho-spirituality: humanistic and transpersonal psychologies, the Growth Movement, the proliferation of self-transformation seminars, and so on—all of these fuse psychological and spiritual techniques of transformation. Whether drawn from the east or the west, psychologically powerful processes such as meditations and psychotherapies are put to the service of self-enlightenment.

Bhagwan has done as much as anyone to encourage this fusion. Rooted in India he has drawn on a whole range of western techniques—encounter, primal, gestalt, bio-energetics, Rolfing, to name but a few. He has done as much as anyone to turn psychology into religion, and religion into psychology. When asked to convey the essence of Bhagwan's method of teaching, we refer people to what he has to say about the fusion:

> This whole life is a challenge to growth. That is the true religion and true psychology, too—because a true religion cannot be other than a true psychology. I call that psychology 'the psychology of the Buddhas'. It gives you a great challenge to be more than you are. It gives you a divine discontent. It makes you aflame with a desire to go higher and higher—not higher than others but higher than yourself.

As for the teaching itself, another short statement suffices:

> I declare to you your Buddhahood. Each person is born to be a Buddha. Less than that won't do.

For him we are all Gods. Like many other contemporary spiritual teachers he claims that we do not know this because we are trapped by our personalities. What he calls the 'ego' is the devil. This is the apparatus which creates all that is negative and which prevents us from living the blissful, celebratory, energized life provided by the God within. Christians might well throw up their hands in horror. The elevation of the inner self to God is in direct conflict with the doctrine of the Fall and the theme of transcendence. But we are not writing from any particular religious viewpoint. For us, Bhagwan's path is important because it epitomizes all those contemporary teachings which do not look any further than the self to find divinity.

Taking Bhagwan's movement seriously is one thing. Doing justice to it is another. Sannyasins have continually told us, 'essentials cannot be talked about'. The path, they say, is about 'experience': 'Sitting on the sidelines and talking about it is a waste of time.' As non-sannyasins we have had to grapple with the problem of trying to convey experiences which we have not had. In an effort to counter this problem we include as many testimonies and statements as possible, both from Bhagwan and from his sannyasins. We allow participants ample opportunity to speak for themselves. Material has been culled from a number of Bhagwan's 350 or so books and from videos. Testimonies and other information have been obtained through fieldwork. Since 1979 one of the authors has spent considerable time mixing with sannyasins in Lancaster, Suffolk (living at the Medina commune), Oregan (visiting Bhagwan's headquarters), and in more everyday settings. At Medina this involved working alongside sannaysins in the laundry, the garden, the print works, the kitchen, and the cleaning department.

Sannyasins will object that however much we rely on what they say, however much we attempt to participate in their lives, we do not get any closer to the heart of their path. In particular, they will object that we are too serious in our enquiry. Sannyasins do not like the intellect. They do not like the seriousness generated by the intellectual struggle of trying to sort out words to describe what is going on. For them the path is spontaneous, playful, and joyous. They would not dream of attempting to do what we do in the following pages.

One last introductory point. For stylistic reasons our account of Bhagwan and his movement is not continually qualified by remarks of the kind 'or so it is believed'. Instead of writing 'sannyasins believe they are moving from the periphery of their being to their Buddhahood', for example, we simply report the belief 'they are on the path of moving from . . .'. Ethnographically speaking, this is true. Whether they are 'really' on any such path is of course another matter.

1

Bhagwan's Path: 'The Unfolding Vision'

We are here in His grace,
Watching His vision unfolding.

Rajneeshee invocation

Bhagwan was born in Kuchwada in 1931. Not surprisingly for an Indian, Bhagwan believes in reincarnation. This is not his first life on earth. Far less usually for an Indian, Bhagwan is able to recall his previous lives. We can thus begin our biographical account by going well back in time.

We are told that in his last incarnation, some seven hundred years ago, he was already a spiritual teacher. Nearing death at the age of 106, he embarked upon a 21-day fast. He wanted to obtain enlightenment and thereby escape from the cycle of rebirth. He was killed three days before enlightenment could take place. Bhagwan now sees that this was for the best. It allowed him to be reborn again and to carry on helping others.

On the surface the first twenty-one years of his present existence have been like those of many. At school he appears to have been clever and gifted, particularly in storytelling and art. He also played truant, establishing himself as a rather rebellious leader of his schoolmates. Joshi, a sannyasin biographer, describes him as being 'egotistical, immodest, discourteous and even seditious'.[1] As he grew up, Bhagwan became interested in politics, for a while flirting with socialism, communism, and two nationalist movements, The Indian National Army and Rashtriya Swayamsavek Singh. At nineteen he went to college and read philosophy, interrupting his studies to spend a period in a newspaper office.

The picture is of a gifted, spirited, independent-minded individual growing up in everyday society. Underneath, however, we are told that Bhagwan was continuing the search which had been cut short seven hundred years before. His rebelliousness can be seen as a manifestation of the fact that he was not content with the solutions to life provided by those in authority. Realizing that no one could answer the 'great questions', he sought self-discovery. Bhagwan subjected himself to intensive meditation. He fasted, practised austerities, spent an increasing amount of time alone, and in general, to use his expression, 'worked on himself'.

The outcome was hardly satisfactory: 'nothing was happening'.[2] More accurately, nothing of value appeared to be happening. The one evident result of Bhagwan's search was that he became psychologically disturbed. He had to fight to hold on to his sanity: 'I had to force myself to eat, force myself to drink. I had to knock myself against the wall to feel whether my head was still there or not. Everything had become so inconsistant that even to formulate one sentence was difficult.'

On 21 March 1953 everything changed. Bhagwan became enlightened. On 14 March he 'stopped working on himself'. 'In sheer helplessness' Bhagwan stopped 'expecting something to happen'. It then 'started happening': 'A new energy arose, out of nowhere. It was not coming from any source. It was coming from nowhere and everywhere. It was in the trees and in the rocks and in the sky and the sun and the air—it was so near and so close.' The seven days culminating in full enlightenment took the form of 'tremendous transformation, total transformation'. Bhagwan felt 'very tranquil, calm and collected and centred'. Then on the last day, the experience shifted gear. Bhagwan felt 'the presence of a totally new energy, a new light, a new delight, so intense that it was almost unbearable, as if I was exploding, as if I was going mad with blissfullness. I was blissed-out, stoned.'

Bhagwan 'lost his autobiography'. Becoming a 'non-being', boundaries, distinctions, and mind all dissolving, Bhagwan merged with the cosmos: 'For the first time I was not alone, for the first time I was no more an individual, for the first time the drop had come and fallen into the ocean.' He experienced power: 'Now the whole ocean was mine, I was the ocean. There was no limitation. A tremendous power arose as if I could do anything whatsoever. I was not there, only the power was there.' The experience was of such a form that 'another reality opened its door, another dimension became available':

Bhagwan, 1985, Rajneeshpuram.

Suddenly it was there, the other reality, the separate reality, the really Real, or whatsoever you want to call it—call it God, call it Truth, call it Dhamma, call it Tao, or whatsoever you will.

In one sense his life ends here. The man known as Rajneesh Chandra Mohan 'died'. He became a vehicle for the divine, empty of ego. In another sense his life carried on much as before. It is true that he no longer had to subject himself to the stresses of seekership. What is surprising, however, given the intensity of his experience, is that he felt able to return to everyday life. He completed his BA (1955) and then obtained an MA with distinction in philosophy. Bhagwan went on to teach the subject at Raipur Sanskrit College. In 1960, aged twenty-nine, he became a professor of philosophy at the University of Jabalpur, a post held until 1966.

Bhagwan kept quiet about his experience for a number of years. He explains why: 'If I had declared that I was enlightened, I would have been killed very easily.' However, he did not remain silent on other matters. From 1960 to 1970 he travelled the length and breadth of India, talking, debating, and attracting a good deal of attention for the outspokenness of his views on contemporary matters. As he says, 'With or without reason I was creating controversies and making criticisms. I began to criticize Gandhiji, I began to criticize socialism.'[3] Gandhi, he said was not a truly religious man; he was not one who had realized himself. Rather he was a man of ethics. And, Bhagwan claimed, Gandhi's preoccupation with the poor had hindered their liberation from poverty. As a result, India had turned its back on technology, in reality the only thing that could free her people. Bhagwan believed that only technology could allow his fellow Indians to concern themselves with their spirituality unhampered by the daily quest for physical survival.

His criticisms were not just directed at Gandhi. Traditional religion did not escape his condemnation either. At the Second World Hindu Religion Conference at Patna, Bhagwan incensed the Hindu High Priest, the Shankacharya of Puri. He delivered a scathing indictment of established religion. In his speech he averred that religion is

an art that shows how to enjoy life. Liberation is not in running away from life, but rather in enjoying fully the life and the world. But the shops which are being run in the name of religion do not want a person to become truly religious.[4]

Nor did Bhagwan limit his energies to attacking mainstream institutions. Despite the fact that he remained quiet about his enlightenment during the 1960s, he began to adopt the role of spiritual master. In 1964 he initiated 'meditation camps' to help others obtain what he himself had experienced. Beginning with quiet meditations, Bhagwan realized that they were inappropriate to the needs of modern man:

> Man is neurotic. The old meditation techniques do not take this into consideration. They can calm you down; your surface can become more peaceful. But nothing really happens to your inner being. The forces, the neurotic forces, will go on boiling within. Any day they will erupt and disturb the surface. [5]

Accordingly in April 1970 he introduced Dynamic Meditation, a technique based on the principle that cathartic activity of an intense kind is needed before inner peace can be attained.

This same year, 1970, was particularly significant. Bhagwan decided to stop his hectic country-ranging lifestyle and settle down. Feeling that he had sown the seeds from which fruit would grow, he took up permanent residence in Bombay. There, for the first time, he began to initiate disciples. It is interesting to note that Prasad, his biographer for the period immediately prior to the Bombay phase, reported Bhagwan as having no such initiatory intentions: 'Rajneesh does not believe in admitting disciples or in founding Institutes for the Harmonious Development of Man.' [6] Nevertheless, the Neo-Sannyas International Movement was established. In the same year Bhagwan also began to hold evening discourses for disciples, speaking in Hindi on a wide variety of spiritual topics.

Throughout the 1960s Bhagwan had been known by the title 'Acharya', meaning teacher, imparter of knowledge. In 1971 he decided to change his designation to one more suited to his new role as spiritual master. 'Bhagwan' can be translated as 'God self-realized' or, more simply, as 'the Blessed One'. This change in title, he explained, mirrored the change in his focus of attention. By now he was concentrating on his relationship with his disciples. Less and less was he accepting invitations to speak publicly. His goal was not to communicate ideas as an Acharya but to change those around him on a much deeper level, through an inner communion. In his words: 'Now I've changed my function absolutely. I have started working on a different level, in a different dimension. Now I give you being, not knowledge. I am going to give you knowing—and that is totally different.' [7]

During the first year of the Neo-Sannyas International Movement he attracted many Indians, his mother among them. Those who took sannyas were largely drawn from the people who had been attending the meditation camps. By the end of 1971 he had also begun to attract a small Western following, people who had to cope with the fact that the discourses were conducted in Hindi. Many of the Westerners lived on a work farm located near Bombay. Veetrag describes the lifestyle: 'There was nothing to do except work. There was no need to think, work was the main thing. The entire focus was on work with the spirit of surrender. People did react to the conditions strongly, but they also learned how to live in a commune in love and acceptance.' [8]

These early sannyasins enjoyed quite informal relationships with Bhagwan. Joshi talks of how they could see him at almost any time of day and of how their encounters with him were both personal and intense. It seemed as if they were being specifically nurtured to provide the foundations for his later work. Among their number was one who was to become his close companion and who was to devote herself to caring for his increasingly fragile body, Ma Yoga Vivek. She was, according to Bhagwan, none other than a reincarnation of his childhood sweetheart, Shashi. (Shashi had died of typhoid in 1947.) A fellow sannyasin describes Vivek and her role as follows:

> A female energy sitting beside him and walking behind him. Behind one set of closed doors she is the housewife/housekeeper/nursemaid who sees that his food is well prepared, his robes washed, his body healthy. Behind another set of closed doors she is . . . what?

In reply to the question 'What do you do with Vivek?' Bhagwan answered:

> I am killing her slowly. That is the only way for her to get a totally new being, to be reborn. It is a cross to be with me. You ask what I'm doing with her? I'm crucifying her, slowly. [9]

Despite the caring of Vivek and others, however, Bhagwan's health began to deteriorate. In particular his asthma and diabetes worsened and it was felt that he should move to a more congenial climate. Anyway, the increase in the numbers of his followers made it desirable that a larger site should be found for a permanent community. Accordingly, Ma Yoga Laxmi, his personal secretary, his very first sannyasin, and the individual who had organized the Neo-Sannyas Movement under his guidance since its birth, was sent to find a new location. Poona was chosen. A site in one of its most prestigious suburbs was bought early in 1974 with money donated to a trust fund by wellwishers and sannyasins.

For a while it seems that the focus of this community differed little from the past. The practical aspects of Bhagwan's teaching still emphasized the value of meditative techniques. Meditation camps were still regularly held, though ill health prevented Bhagwan from directing them in person: an empty chair was placed on the podium to symbolize his presence. The working lives of the sannyasins were modelled on the prototype Bombay commune which had by now been disbanded. Yet the seeds of enormous change were in the air. The movement was on the brink of a massive explosion in terms of the numbers of westerners attracted to Bhagwan.

During the later 1970s some 30,000 people from all over the world visited the ashram each year. [10] At any one time there would be more than 6,000 sannyasins at Poona. The explosion in numbers was largely due to the fact that Bhagwan introduced activities which appealed to many in the west. In April 1975 the first therapy groups began. Poona rapidly became known as the place to go for radical psychotherapy. Bhagwan's name and teachings became established on the new age 'growth circuit'. The effect he had on westerners who came across him convinced others that Poona was the place to go. Well-known and influential group therapy leaders from Europe and America spread the message that Bhagwan highlighted the limitations of their previous work. They spread the message that he provided an opportunity to expand into the spiritual dimension. As Joshi says,

> They came to learn from him how to be meditative. They found him to be the only spiritual master who fully understood the concept of holistic psychology, and the one who could use it as a means of bringing individuals to higher levels of meditativeness. [11]

The 'Buddhafield' at Poona pleased those in the growth culture who wanted to try out as many ways as possible for developing human potential. As Bhagwan describes it, Poona provided a 'gigantic experiment':

> My ashram is a lab, we experiment here. That is creating great trouble because man has forgotten to experiment. We are experimenting in a multi-dimensional way. We are experimenting with Sufism, we are experimenting with Jainism, Hinduism, Islam, Christianity; we are experimenting with Tao, Tantra, Yoga, alchemy. We are experimenting

with all the possibilities that can make the human consciousness whole and a human being rich. So this is a new experiment; it has never been done before in such a way. This is a synthesis of all the paths. [12]

It was an experiment in all the techniques that could possibly be used to provoke Buddhahood. New ideas were being introduced all the time. Some, like Dynamic Meditation, were adopted as valuable on a permanent basis. Others were seen as having a place in the ashram as short-term measures, such as tratak and kirtan meditation techniques. [13] Once their usefulness was considered to be at an end they were discarded.

Sannyasins who decided to stay and work in the ashram had their food and accommodation provided. A minority lived within the confines of the ashram itself, but with space being severely restricted most lived outside in the city. Nevertheless, a strong sense of group attunement began to be experienced. This was felt to emanate from Bhagwan. Gradually it infused the body of disciples and was felt to transform their daily activities: 'In a spiritual commune there is no longer any work; it is only allowing something to happen through you. The work acquires an aesthetic quality, and a climate is created for everyone to fall into harmony together.' [14]

Their 'work' included editing discourses to be made into books, cleaning toilets, accountancy and finance, cooking, advertising, gardening, and washing down Bhagwan's cars. Whatever their chore, work was seen as an opportunity to be near the Master and fully involved in what was happening. Perhaps the dominant experience was of abundance. Simant, with whom we have talked, describes it thus:

Working in the ashram for the first few years was like Christmas every day. In Poona that wasn't to do with getting a free pass to go to morning discourse every day, or anything material. But Christmas for me, having come from a large family, was gifts showering all around. And every day in Poona I experienced that feeling of abundance, of being showered with all my heart's desire.

All who were there saw the period as one in which they were forced to examine their assumptions about themselves and the world in which they lived. It was an exhilarating and intense time:

The ashram is crazy, it's chaotic. It's the exact kind of ashram Bhagwan should have, and the kind of ashram that no other Master but he could have. It's a funhouse and a madhouse. A bawdyhouse and a temple. There's music and dancing and laughter. There's silence and reverence and stillness.

It was seen by the Westerners as a place unlike any other in the world. It challenged in an exciting new way the traditional image of a religious community. It was, for them, a spiritual bazaar offering an ever-changing variety of techniques and experiences in response to the moment, with at its core a guru, an extraordinary and charismatic man.

Each day would formally begin at 6 a.m. with Dynamic Meditation. The streets around Koregaon Park where the ashram was situated would be flooded with orange-clad sannyasins interspersed with ordinarily dressed visitors making their way to the ornate entrance. Later in the morning Bhagwan would be driven to Buddha Hall from his own residence a hundred yards away in one of an increasing number of Rolls Royces at his disposal. He then delivered a two-hour or so spontaneous lecture. The lectures covered a wide spectrum of subjects. He would provide long answers to questions, provide commentaries on other religious traditions, observations on well-known individuals or on contemporary events and issues, and would also, of course, provide a liberal sprinkling of jokes. He would then be driven back, and the crowds which had gathered to hear him speak would disperse, either to attend to work in and around the ashram, to participate in a group or a meditation, or perhaps simply to eat, drink, and soak up the atmosphere around them. The day would draw to a close with 'darshan' with the Master, opportunities for small numbers of sannyasins to meet and talk with him one-to-one. If going back to the West they would take their leave of him there. Otherwise most sannyasins would go to discuss problems or to ask which groups and meditations were particularly suitable for them.

In addition to this daily routine, four major celebrations were held each year when the numbers at the ashram would swell still further. These were held on the day of Bhagwan's enlightenment (21 March), on Guru Purnima Day, a traditional day of celebration when disciples in India acknowledge their relationship with their Master (6 July), on Bhagwan's birthday (11 December), and on Mahaparinirvana Day (8 September). This last was to celebrate all those sannyasins who had died, special attention being paid to sannyasins whom Bhagwan declared had become enlightened on dying. These included his own (biological) father and Prince Welf of Hanover, who had been among his first sannyasins.

Poona might have been considered a 'funhouse' and a 'madhouse', but it was far from being unregulated. There were numerous rules.

Certain areas were restricted for the use of ashram residents. Smoking was not allowed on the premises and neither were drugs. There were guards on the gate where those entering the ashram were enjoined to leave their 'shoes and their minds' and where everyone going to lectures or darshans with Bhagwan had their hair sniffed. Those whose hair smelt were turned away, at least half a dozen on some occasions. This, it was said, was to protect Bhagwan who was sensitive to smell and highly allergic. Other rules for darshan included not going nearer than a metre to Bhagwan and the necessity of making an appointment first.

The environment provided a context for transformation. It facilitated surrender to the master's path. Bhagwan was very much in 'control,' saying: 'Nothing is out of my hands. What is happening at the ashram is exactly what's supposed to happen. If you want to surrender to me, you have to surrender to what's happening around me.' [15] Thus Bhagwan often decided who was to work at what and which of the therapies or meditations his sannyasins should take. He also commented on relationships and was seen to be responsible for major policy decisions.

From 1979 contact with Bhagwan declined. The early evening darshans changed from being meetings to being 'energy darshans'. No longer were those present allowed to converse with him. Instead, Bhagwan would press on their psychic centre, their 'third eye', on the forehead. It was explained that in so doing he was transmitting his energy to his followers. Using his own words, Bhagwan was moving his sannyasins into the dimension of knowing rather than knowledge; of communion rather than communication. This change heralded another period of radical transition which put his relationship with his sannyasins on a new footing.

This phase was probably precipitated by Bhagwan's failing health, for in June 1979 he was forced to stop both darshans and discourses for a short time. During this period sannyasins attended silent meditations, accompanied by music, reputedly experiencing for themselves what Bhagwan meant by their having heart-to-heart communion with him. The period lasted ten days. By the ninth day, 'The energy had mounted to a crescendo in his eloquent presence. It was as if he were entering each one of us, feeling and sensing who could be with him without the need of words.' [16] On the eleventh day, Bhagwan resumed speaking.

Around this time, plans were being drawn up for a new site for the ashram. Bhagwan was formulating a more complex vision, that of constructing a new kind of commune. He wanted this to be in his home territory:

> India is becoming like a wound, a cancer. I see all this. That's why I don't want to leave this country. I want to create a small oasis, a commune, which will be absolutely technological and still ecological. It will be a totally different kind of communism. It can be of much help, it can create much inspiration. [17]

A location was chosen for this enterprise, to be named Rajneeshdham, at Jadhawadi, Saswad. Four hundred acres were to be used to accommodate an agricultural commune based on meditation and love.

Then, on 10 April 1981, a message was sent out to the community both in Poona and abroad:

> We are happy to announce that a new and ultimate phase has started in Bhagwan's work. Bhagwan was waiting for the right time and number of his people to get ready and that has happened, so now he can start his invisible work. It is time for him to be silent so that he can approach us more deeply. [18]

His sannyasins were told that his representatives would attend darshans in his stead and that morning celebrations, heart-to-heart communions called 'satsangs', would be held in place of daily discourses. Bhagwan would no longer speak in public. He had withdrawn, it was said, so that he could focus his attention on his inner work. By excluding the unnecessary he could operate at a much more potent and creative pace.

Preparations for moving the ashram to Saswad continued. However, on 27 May there was a fire at Rajneeshdham. Following on the heels of this apparent setback, and despite repeated assertions that he would never leave India, Bhagwan flew to America on 1 June 1981.

For a short time the vast majority of his sannyasins had no idea of Bhagwan's whereabouts. To all intents and purposes he had completely disappeared. Speculation ended when he reappeared in New Jersey, wearing, according to one unsubstantiated report, a T-shirt emblazoned with the words 'INDIA. TAKE IT OR LEAVE IT'. On the back was written 'I LEFT IT'. Sannyasin representatives reported that he had gone to the USA for medical reasons. In late July 1981 he moved to a small sannyasin community in Oregon (this had been set up earlier the same month). In keeping with its ill-fated predecessor, the community was to be a model for the future, based on agriculture and with a city for its workers. The city is called Rajneeshpuram; the surrounding land is known as The Big Muddy Ranch.

The journey to Oregon appears to have resulted in an expansion of the movement. A spokeswoman at Rajneeshpuram, speaking in 1983, claimed that Bhagwan's following had grown. Rajneeshpuram itself was by now well established, with some 2,000 members. A network of communes was being developed in many countries. including England, where the main centre was Medina. Each centre was modelled on Rajneeshpuram. Each embodied the spirit of Bhagwan's teaching.

Wanting to stay in America, Bhagwan became embroiled in a struggle with US Immigration officials to gain permanent residency. Lawsuit followed lawsuit. Letters flooded in from around the world testifying to his influence as a spiritual figure. Finally there came the revelation that Bhagwan had long ago been adopted by an Indian couple who had become permanent residents of America in 1973. A week later, Bhagwan was reluctantly granted the first part of his visa application. He was accorded the status of a religious leader, provisionally able to continue his pastoral work.

Another development bound up with the move to America involved the remoulding of the Neo-Sannyas Movement. On 5 December 1981 it was proclaimed that all sannyasins were henceforth members of an organized religion. Ma Anand Sheela, who had by this time taken over the role of personal secretary to Bhagwan from Ma Yoga Laxmi, informed his disciples that 'a new religion has been born called Rajneeshism. A sannyasin can also be called a Rajneeshee.' [19] A short book (*Rajneeshism*, 1983) provides an explanation of why it had come to be felt that Bhagwan's vision should be more systematically formulated than it had been in the past. As the author (probably Sheela) wrote:

> The enlightened Master, Bhagwan Shree Rajneesh, has often said that religious experience cannot be expressed in words. Any attempt to conceptualize it, define it, or explain it is bound to fail.
>
> Given this fact, many Masters in the past did not create a canon of religious doctrine while they were alive. They worked directly with their disciples, trying to awaken in them the experience of enlightenment.
>
> After they had gone, well-intentioned disciples created doctrines around their teachings, forming religious organizations to interpret,

clarify and spread the message. These organizations were developed from fragments of the teachings of the Masters, which had been recollected, compiled and enshrined by well-meaning but unenlightened followers.

Seeing the inevitability of this process, Bhagwan Shree Rajneesh is giving His spiritual direction to disciples who are creating a religion which will accurately reflect His teaching—while He is still alive. This religion is known as Rajneeshism.[20]

The religion, then, is meant to provide a clearer and more comprehensive statement of the path. At the organizational level a ministry was introduced, overseen by the Academy of Rajneeshism. A considerable number of the developments had to do with ministerial duties. Once qualified, activities performed by particular ministers depended on the kind of 'energy' they possess. 'Arihantas', those whose 'basic energy is outgoing, extroverted', are best able to 'reach the state of godliness through serving others'. They thus performed the newly introduced marriage and birth ceremonies. 'Siddhas', whose energy 'is basically introverted', are best able to reach godliness by 'working on themselves'. They were 'empowered to perform' the sannyasin death ceremony. Finally 'Acharyas', combining both forms of energy, could perform all three kinds of ceremonies, as well as being 'empowered to initiate new disciples into Neo-Sannyas'.

Sannyasins no longer had to turn to other religions to sacralize their marriages. This illustrates that Rajneeshism was a 'new' religion. However, none of the religious practices associated with it were without precedents from earlier days. In the past, darshan, the evening meeting, could only be held in the Master's presence. Now all that had to be present was the 'being of the Master'. Darshan involves 'singing, dancing and melting, a state of utter drunkeness'. Satsang, first introduced in Poona as a replacement to morning discourse, also served as a silent, heart-to-heart communion with Bhagwan's 'presence'. It is inspired by readings from his books, music, and a humming meditation. A final development is that every sannyasin is asked to kneel and chant a ritual, first performed solely by disciples at Poona but now extended to all. Gachchhamis are practiced at the start and close of day. The ritual consists of repeating three sentences in Sanskrit:

Buddham Sharanam Gachchhami.
Sangham Sharanam Gachchhami.
Dhammam Sharanam Gachchhami.

Translated into English this runs:

> I go to the feet of the Awakened One.
> I go to the feet of the Commune of the Awakened One.
> I go to the feet of the Ultimate Truth of the Awakened One. [21]

Apart from developing Rajneeshism, Bhagwan stirred things up in other ways. 1984 turned out to be an eventful year. The authors of this book were fortunate enough to be present when the first bombshell was dropped. We had been invited to a meeting to listen to Sheela, Bhagwan's mouthpiece, who was beginning a European tour. Five hundred or so sannyasins sat in a crowded hotel room in London to hear the news from Oregon. Having shown three videos of Rajneeshpuram, Sheela invited questions. Only one was answered, for suddenly Sheela started talking about AIDS. She had shown Bhagwan three photographs of sannyasins who had died of the virus. Bhagwan had replied that this was the plague prophesied by Nostradamus; the plague that would wipe out the majority of the world's population. Bhagwan went on to say that the disease had already struck half the population of Africa, where it had originated, and was soon to wipe out two thirds of humanity.

Sheela's message, relayed from Bhagwan, was that AIDS must not be allowed to destroy his work. Bhagwan had three specific solutions to offer his sannyasins. The ideal solution is quite simple: be celibate. If that does not seem natural, then follow the second solution: practice fidelity. If you have been faithful for over two years it is safe to have sex. But if you desire sex before that, or if you are unattached and casual about sex, then you must follow a strict code of behaviour. This solution lies with disposable gloves (for contact below the waist), with condoms, with no oral or anal sex, with no communal bathing or jacuzzis. Finally, the sannyasins were told that homosexual and lesbian behaviour was largely out of the question.

At a time when little was known of the disease in this country, the announcement came as a shock to Sheela's audience. (Outsiders were also surprised, given the movement's reputation as a sex cult.) On their return to Medina and other centres, sannyasins were faced with neatly laid out rubber gloves and condoms. Their reactions will be discussed later. AIDS-related restrictions on behaviour have since increased. A message was soon received from Oregon stating that two years was not long enough to render a relationship safe. Couples should now take precautions (wearing rubber gloves and the rest) for six years. A sterilizing agent should be used for rinsing food utensils. Kissing has been banned. Hugging remains allowed: the last vestige of sensual freedom.

Another eventful occurrence in 1984 was the revelation that over a period of days in July twenty sannyasins had become enlightened. The efficacy of the path had apparently been demonstrated, for previously none of the followers of Bhagwan had been acknowledged as fully realizing their Buddhahood. In early 1985, however, Bhagwan said that attaining enlightenment is not like becoming qualified for inclusion on an honours list. He said that he had only been joking.

The Rajneesh Times (British edition) of November 1984 reported the next major development of the year:

> As softly as a door opens and as spontaneously as a bird takes flight, Bhagwan Shree Rajneesh has begun to speak again. After 1,315 days of silence, Bhagwan has started a series of special talks on October 30 1984, entitled The Rajneesh Bible. [22]

One reason given for Bhagwan breaking his silence is that he wanted to put some 'finishing touches' to his teaching. He also felt that the time had come for him to talk directly to his sannyasins. His sannyasins, he said, had developed to a point where they could be told 'the whole truth'. His disciples responded with joy. Not many were especially surprised: sannyasins are well accustomed to Bhagwan's mercurial temperament. For their Master to break a vow of perpetual silence is par for the course.

For sannyasins living in Britain, the final significant event of 1984 came in December. Members of the smaller sannyasin centres, around twenty in all, were asked to move to Medina. Sannyasins flooded in from Sangeet in Leeds, Gourishankar in Edinburgh, Udgatri in Bristol, and from the others. Businesses were hurriedly sold and Medina was swamped by the influx. Numbers there were further swelled by sannyasins from outside the centres deciding to move in as well. Then later in the month the news broke that Medina itself was to close as a fully-fledged commune. Inhabitants were told that they should leave Britain and join communities on the continent. The only exceptions to this were parents of children under five (who had permission to remain at Medina) and sannyasins remaining there as teachers and helpers. Medina was to become a school for sannyasin children living in Europe. As of December 1984 the school catered for approximately 150 children, ranging in age from six months to sixteen years.

The year 1984 ended with change in the air. Sannyasins were

leaving the UK, making for Europe and larger centres such as those in Berlin, Cologne, and Hamburg. Without a centre in Britain the 4,000 sannyasins who have stayed in this country have had to live alone or in small households. In the absence of a focal point they have to rely on inspiration from Rajneeshpuram. During 1985, however, even this focal point was subject to radical change: this year was in fact the most tumultuous period in the history of the movement. Change became so radical that we can only assume that sannyasins' love of the unexpected was stretched to the limit. [23]

So what has happened? Change appears to have been precipitated by the abrupt departure of Bhagwan's personal secretary, Ma Anand Sheela, together with a renegade group of fifteen, including the mayor of Rajneeshpuram and the president of the international organization. Leaving for West Germany in mid-September 1985, Sheela and her group have been directing accusation after accusation at the man to whom they had previously surrendered as the embodiment of the divine. Sheela has been behaving rather like a disillusioned lover. Her attraction to Bhagwan she now says had little to do with spirituality. She had worked to win his love. She left, as she puts it, 'because I could no longer bear the incredible pressure of running the commune 18 hours a day to provide Rajneesh with Rolls-Royce cars, diamond watches, jewellery'. Sheela had become sick of pandering to the whims of 'a liar and a crook'. [24]

Sheela says that she had become aware of abuses within the community. Among other things she mentions drug taking and dealing at the Ranch, this serving to keep sannyasins compliant and to make money. Bhagwan himself, she says, was never without his pills and thrived on laughing gas. She also alleges that AIDS victims had been deliberately brought into the community to frighten off unwelcome visitors. One final accusation is that Rajneeshism only has a tenth of the followers it has been claiming.

Bhagwan has not let these accusations go unchallenged. His side of the story is that Sheela had been busy establishing her own 'facist regime' within the commune. Sheela has been the witch within. Her claim that she has been implementing his orders are rubbish; indeed she has attempted to poison Bhagwan, his doctor, and the D.A. In addition, Sheela attempted to wipe out a neighbouring non-sannyasin community by contaminating the water supply. She is also accused of keeping the community under close scrutiny by introducing bugging devices, of arming sannyasins loyal to her, and of fleecing the commune of some 55 million dollars.

More fundamentally, Bhagwan claims that Sheela instigated the transformation of his spiritual path of freedom into the doctrinally and ritually laden religion of Rajneeshism. As he has recently said, 'I teach independence. Be skeptical.' It is Sheela, the 'reborn Adolf Hitler', motivated by jealousy and a lust for power, who has been saying 'believe, surrender'. It is Sheela who says that 'all these things', from guns to Rajneeshism, 'are coming from Bhagwan'. The organized religion, it appears, is Sheela's way of implementing control.

Bhagwan has thus tried to detach himself from some of the excesses and disruptions which have recently afflicted the community. To underline his detachment he has systematically demolished what he now claims to be Sheela's creations. 'Rajneeshism is dead', is the new cry. Six thousand copies of the book which first spelt out this religion were burnt (the ritual occurred at the end of September). The priests have gone. Disciples have been told that they no longer need to wear orange clothes, or even a mala.

The path appears to be returning to the original free, spontaneous, anti-religious spirit of the movement. As the following statement of Bhagwan's indicates, Sheela's power-trip is now being treated as part of the teaching. It provides a lesson in what corrupts freedom. Sannyasins world wide have now watched a video during which Bhagwan tells them, 'Just watch one thing: that you are not dominating anybody. You are not being dominated by anyone. You are a free individual.' Bhagwan continues, clearly referring to Sheela and her associates, 'I am not angry with them. I am not against them. They have shown sannyasins that these [power and privilege] are the poisons that corrupt.' And Bhagwan closes with how things are going to change:

> Now we are going to decentralize. And the people in power will be changed over often. Every person in power has to understand he is a servant of the commune, not the master. [25]

More recently still, the return to the roots has taken an extremely literal form. Bhagwan has returned to India. As with the demolition of Rajneeshism, the events leading up to this appear to be largely fortuitous, outside the control of Bhagwan. For reasons which are as yet unclear, but which probably owe much to information which Sheela has been supplying to the authorities, Bhagwan recently attempted to leave the USA. His plane, en route to Bermuda, was grounded by immigration officials who had been been monitoring his flight by radar. Placed in jail in North Carolina with a dozen close followers, Bhagwan was charged with a number of offences (available figures range from 35 to 500). After a week the living Buddha obtained bail for half a million dollars and returned to Rajneeshpuram. He then struck a deal with the authorities. He admitted one charge, to do with circumventing immigration laws by arranging marriages, and paid a fine. (It should be pointed out that Bhagwan immediately claimed his innocence.) In return Bhagwan was allowed to leave the country. As of writing Bhagwan is back in a small village in northern India living with a few disciples at a spot 'where the snow has not melted sinced the Buddha's day'.

In September 1985 Bhagwan said that he was 'an ordinary man'. He is today even more 'an ordinary man', at least in the sense of doing away with the trappings of high position. The Rolls Royces, which for a long time provided the only setting in which most sannyasins would see their Master, are now (as of March 1986) all sold. Having cast off the burdens of office, or, as some might say, having had them cast from him, Bhagwan could even be said to be recuperating.

As for the situation in England, Medina has now been sold—to a traditional Buddhist order!

Three months have elapsed since we completed this book at the close of 1985—time for plenty to happen in what must be one of the least predictable of new religious movements.

Bhagwan is no longer in India. With the Indian government refusing to extend the tourist visas of a number of his personal household, and instructing overseas consulates not to issue visas to sannyasins, Bhagwan apparently felt it appropriate to move. Flying to Crete after a spell in Nepal (Kathmandu), he stayed at the villa of a Greek film director. It did not take long for Bhagwan to incense members of the Orthodox Church, to the extent that clergymen threatened to stone sannyasins (some eight hundred had gathered on the island). Perceived as a 'menace to public safety', and with his own tourist visa revoked, Bhagwan was deported in early March. He then spent eighteen hours at Heathrow (7 March). Refused entry by officers at the airport, apparently because of 'undesirability in view of American convictions', Bhagwan left for Ireland, more specifically for Jury's Hotel, Limerick. On 19 March he changed abode yet again, arriving in Uruguay after having been refused landing permission at Antigua.

Bhagwan's future whereabouts is clearly uncertain. He has recently been refused visas by Sweden, Switzerland, and Spain, as well as by the United Kingdom and Antigua. Sannyasins themselves are talking of his 'world tour'. With no signs of Bhagwan establishing another focal commune, and with much of the old organization being dismantled, the path awaits new developments. Rajneeshpuram, now run by a skeleton staff, is for sale; central organizations are no longer important. Publishing houses have stopped functioning. The movement's headquarters, such as it is, is based in Poona again (where would-be converts now have to write to obtain permission to take sannyas). Communes in Germany, more alive than elsewhere, are being run on an 'autonomous' basis. Overall, the picture is of sannyasins being left more to themselves, with Bhagwan emphasizing that he is a 'friend', not a 'master', and discoursing (in Crete) on 'not following me', and mixing with his sannyasins, when possible, in a free and easy fashion.

Another development worthy of note is that Sheela, together with two other female sannyasins, was arrested in West Germany early in 1985. Extradicated to Oregon, she is currently in prison awaiting trial. Sheela and Puja (the former head of the Rajneesh Medical Corporation) have been charged by a Federal grand jury of 'conspiracy to tamper with consumer products'. More exactly, they are charged with causing an outbreak of food poisoning. They are alleged to have contaminated food in ten restaurants in The Dalles (a community near Rajneeshpuram) in order to prevent opponents voting in a local election. As a result over 750 people are held to have fallen ill. Partly because of evidence provided by Krishna Deva (formerly Mayor of Rajneeshpuram, one-time member of Sheela's group, now chief prosecution wittness), Sheela is also accused of having attempted to murder Bhagwan's personal physician (Swami Devaraj), of extensive wire tapping on the Ranch, and of organizing immigration violations.

The outcome of the court case could obviously have a bearing on the future of Bhagwan and his path. But this aside, are there any signs of the way in which things might develop? Our guess is that the path will move into a phase more akin to earlier days. Sannyasins are talking of smaller communes and centres. With Bhagwan teaching that sannyasins should not depend on him as an authoritative, infallible god, the emphasis seems likely to become more experiential; more to do with self-discovery than with guru worship. That, at least, is how sannysins in England tend to see the future. And perhaps it is not without significance that the newly-established, sannyasin-run, therapy centre in London, providing many experiental groups, is called Quaesitor II; for it was people from Quaesitor, the growth centre founded in 1969, who were attracted to Bhagwan's path and who were to become leading figures in what they saw as a way to self-realization.

2

The Teaching:
'Off With Your Heads'

*Only if you are ready to drop the ego,
your judgements, and your rationality,
your intellect—only if you are ready to
allow me to cut off your head—will you be
able to understand what is happening here.*

Bhagwan Shree Rajneesh

Bhagwan's teaching is radical. It is radical in its nature, for it is not held to involve anything to do with ideas; and it is radical in its goal, for it is aimed at effecting nothing less than the transformation of what it is to be human. Both these characteristics are aptly summed up by Bhagwan himself when he says, 'I am not teaching you an ideology, and I am not teaching you an anti-ideology. I am teaching you a way of being, a different quality of existence.' [1]

Bhagwan is scathing of those who would use their intellects or minds to follow his path. The intellect can only understand concepts and ideas, structures and ideologies. It is therefore useless if the aim is that of experiencing a 'quality of existence' which lies beyond the mind. It is true that what he calls 'inauthentic religion' can be grasped by our normal ways of understanding things. But inauthentic religions, such as Christianity, are the products of mental activities which block off the authentic:

> Authentic religion is an enquiry into what is. Inauthentic religion
> is inventive. Mind invents. And mind is the barrier. And once mind
> invents, it only creates great philosophies: Christianity, Hinduism,
> Judaism. [2]

Authentic religious life, as conveyed by Bhagwan, must be approached by discarding the intellect. Bhagwan's utterances are those of a mystic, unable to do more than hint at the truth. His aim is to conjure up that which cannot be intellectually understood. His utterances are not to be taken literally, for they are aimed at evoking that *totality* of experience which goes beyond all words. His utterances thus have to be provisional, for how can any word, or any combination of words, hope to capture life as totality? Furthermore, his utterances have to be contradictory:

> You are morbid if you are confined to anything—whatsoever the name. If opposites meet in you, you become perfect. That's why a perfect man can never be consistent. He has to be contradictory. What to say about God ?—vast! He contains all contradictions. [3]

Since God 'contains all contradictions', the contradictory nature of Bhagwan's teaching is appropriate to his purpose of evoking the experience of God. And of course by being contradictory Bhagwan stops his followers from relying too much on their minds. The mind finds contradictions hard to understand.

We have to provide an outline of the teaching. It is all very well for Bhagwan to state that 'Once you become dependent on borrowed light, you are lost. Knowing is good, but knowledge is not good. Knowing is yours, knowledge is others.' [4] We have somehow to use our largely academic skills to make sense of what we must treat as 'knowledge'. We also have to try and handle the intellectually disturbing presence of contradictions by identifying the more stable of Bhagwan's 'beliefs' and showing how they hang together. Let us but try.

To begin with, the essence of the teaching has to do with what Bhagwan takes to be the natural state of humanity; with what he considers to be the ultimate reality of human existence. All hinges on one fundamental assumption: quite simply, we are all Buddhas. We are all divine; or, to put it another way, the Kingdom of Heaven dwells within us all.

Bhagwan in fact employs a variety of terms to describe the Buddha within. He talks of God, Brahman, Truth, the Void, Totality, Samadhi, Beingness, and Non-Being. He also employs a range of terms to describe how the divine can manifest itself in human experience and action. He talks of bliss, love, joy, detachment, authenticity, freedom, naturalness, spontaneity, and emptiness. He talks of the genuinely religious person acting out of a choiceless awareness, with complete spontaneity and fulfilment; he talks of celebration; he talks of being that which you really are, being yourself, absolutely, authentically and without effort.

Above all, perhaps, he talks of the consequences of living a true life:

> Be true and you will be blissful. Be authentic and you will be happy.

And that happiness will be uncaused. It will just be a part of your being true.[5]

Another favourite theme, which captures well the paradoxical nature of the teaching, is that the ground of our being is empty, yet flowers:

> You transcend all categories, you are just space, and out of that emptiness all these flowers flower. You are flowers of emptiness, forms of nothingness.[6]

Bhagwan has also made the remarkable claim,

> All that exists is divine. Existence is divine; to exist is to be divine.[7]

The claim is remarkable because it suggests that there is no need for Bhagwan to help us in any way. For if all is divine, then all we need to do is to carry on as ever, accepting divinity in everything we do or encounter. There is indeed an aspect of his teaching which appears to say 'all is sacred as it is; there is nothing to be done; simply accept'. Bharti puts it like this:

> It's Bhagwan's acceptance of everything—absolutely, unconditionally—that seems to be the one common thread that runs through all his teachings. Accept yourself, accept life, accept things as they are. The Ganges and sewer water—to Bhagwan, both are equally sacred. He tells us to accept our pains and our frustrations, to accept our non-acceptance.[8]

It seems clear, however, that Bhagwan is not to be taken too literally or seriously when he tells us that '*all* that exists is divine', when he speaks in terms of our accepting *everything*. As the reader might well be thinking, why should we accept our pains and frustrations when there are the joys of Buddhahood to be experienced? How can Bhagwan tell us that all is divine when much of what we encounter and experience patently differs from the bliss of Buddhahood? How can it make sense to talk of Buddhahood as being the realm of the authentic if there is nothing inauthentic with which to contrast it?

It seems clear, in other words, that Bhagwan is working with a two tier model of reality. On the one hand there is the realm of the divine. On the other the realm in which most people live. There must be a spanner in the works, something separate from the divine, to explain why there is a gulf between what we commonly experience in everyday life (not exactly tantamount to bliss and celebration) and the state of Buddhahood. There must be a non-divine level of life and experience to explain why we are not in contact with the

Buddhahood which lies within us all. If there were no spanner in the works we would all be fully fledged Buddhas—and without Bhagwan.

The spanner in the works, it should go without saying, is the mind. The mind (or ego) prevents experience of the god within. 'You are gods and goddesses in exile' is Bhagwan's blunt message.[9] And we are exiled because of our attachment to the mind, ego, the separate and individualized 'I'.

Far from being divine and worthy of 'acceptance', the mind and its products has to go. 'Off with your heads!' Only then can enlightenment occur:

> When the ego is gone the whole individuality arises in its crystal purity: transparent, intelligent, radiant, happy, alive. Vibrating with an unknown rhythm. That unknown rhythm is God.[10]

The important point is that Buddhahood does not have to be acquired, by salvatory or any other means. We are already Buddhas. In the words of Bhagwan,

> Even while you are in the darkest hole of your life, you are still divine. You cannot lose your divinity. I tell you, there is no need for salvation, it is within you.[11]

Rather than being acquired, divinity has to be revealed. The crux of Bhagwan's teaching thus bears on the nature of what stands in the way of revelation, and how this obstacle is to be surmounted. The crux of the teaching has to do with handling the tyrannical hold of the mind.

But why is the mind such a dreadful obstacle? We must now explore Bhagwan's understanding of the nature of the mind, and then introduce the techniques which he provides for exorcising its tyranny. We must look at 'the psychology of the Buddhas'.

Bhagwan's assumption is that the mind is first and foremost a mechanism for survival. It tells us what to do in order to obtain what it deems to be necessary. As a result, we lose contact with ourselves:

> At some point in our childhood we decided that in order to survive, to get the love we needed to exist, it was necessary to stop being ourselves—we had to be the way others, usually our parents, wanted us to be. At that moment we stopped being real and became phoney—and the tragedy is that we have now forgotten the reality! We couldn't allow ourselves to feel, and to stop the feelings we tensed

our bodies, supressed our needs, and stopped breathing.[12]

Bhagwan accepts that the mind is not without use (he writes, for example, that 'we train a child to focus his mind—to concentrate—because without concentration he will not be able to cope with life'[13]). But the compulsion to think in terms of survival extends well beyond practical utilitarian considerations, such as deciding whether or not it is safe to cross a road. As human beings, we also acquire social identities which have to be protected if our 'survival' is not to be threatened.

Parents, schools, religions, institutions in general tell us what we are. All impose on us ways in which we ought to behave and we accept this imposition. We come to believe that if we do not behave in appropriate ways, we no longer are whatever it is we have been defined as being. This situation, says the mind, is a threat to our survival. In response, we find ways of coping, of aspiring to those social expectations of what we should be. We plot and scheme, act deceitfully, to win the approval of others. We believe this to be vital for our continuing security and for our existence as social beings. We need to be loved, so we do things (such as giving to others) to obtain the desired response. We feel that we should not be angry in polite company (for to do so could threaten the identify we want to convey), and so we repress the emotion. In short, we feel that to ignore the mind and its socialized way of operating is to court disaster.

The mind is governed by the twin imperatives of physical and social survival. In accordance with the rule that our identity is at risk if we break with how we should be and is enhanced if we accord with what we feel is expected, the mind attends scrupulously to the dictates of society. The survival strategies which it creates become ingrained in our behaviour. People become more or less completely conditioned; they more or less become automatons, at the mercy of their acquired (and inbuilt) mechanisms of survival. Like Gurdjieff before him, Bhagwan says that in this sense,

> Man is a machine.
> He is born, lives, loves, dies—
> but not as a man;
> he is born, lives, loves, dies
> just like a machine.
> He is not conscious.[14]

This characteristic of the mind, to become fixed in terms of how it has learnt to operate, ensures that we act as though who we are, and how we must proceed if we are to protect and nurture ourselves, is a matter of obeying that great 'god' society. The result is what Bharti describes as 'garbage'. Garbage includes 'Neuroses, suppressions, desires, ambitions, jealousies, angers, fears, ego-trips, body blocks, mind blocks, societal and parental conditioning, accumulated knowledge, accumulated possessions.' [15] The dynamics of the mind ensures that it gets itself in a mess.

According to Bhagwan, one way in which mental processes generate garbage has to do with the fact that the mind naturally gravitates towards whatever it is trying to push away. Consider sexuality. Due to repressive social attitudes towards sexuality, our society as a whole is obsessed with sex. This gravitation, seen in the interest shown in pornography, prostitution, and stories of rape, for example, results in unnatural and unhealthy attitudes. Guilt, neurosis, and the like have become associated with sex, compounding the feeling that it is dirty: 'If you want to understand me, this paradox has to be understood very very deeply, clearly: you have been made sexual by all the condemnation of sex' [16]

Another aspect of the problems deriving from the nature of the mind is that it tends to generate negative rather than positive emotions. Negative emotions are to the fore for several reasons. First, the mind tends to express those feelings deemed socially undesirable. This inevitably generates neurotic energy-consuming states. Secondly, the mind has a natural tendency to seek more of what it enjoys. This means that it is never satisfied, never free of anxiety. We all know the experience of having a good time with, say, a lover, and then wanting more of the same. Our experience of what could simply be something enjoyable is marred by anxiety that we will not be able to sustain it. Again, our desire for power and control means that we are never satisfied we have enough power and are continually afraid of losing what control we might have. Says Bhagwan, 'power and the search for power is mad. It is a madness.' [17] Finally, negative emotions are to the fore because our emotional responses to situations generally take a distorted form. The ego does not like simply to accept and take responsibility for many emotional states. Thus when we feel angry, we tend to blame external events. Balking at simply accepting the feeling, we say 'the fault is with others, not ourselves'. By blaming others for the emotion we get locked into a 'game' which only makes matters worse. Anger grows when we treat ourselves as victims of the actions of others.

As for the relative absence of positive emotions, the main point here is that the mind has established an entity for itself which cuts us off from the source of what is really good about life. The entity is the ego: that 'doer' which has been created to allow us to satisfy our need to think we exercise power and control. In reality, however, the ego isolates us from the rest of existence. The ego means we behave and feel as if we are islands unto ourselves, always trying to turn experience into what we want it to be. It prevents us from simply accepting reality and the flow. To do so would invalidate its own separate identity and its own survival strategy of working in terms of the past in order to gain more power and control in the future.

The mind-ego cuts us adrift from our authentic feelings, the immediacy of what is. As Rajen, in the *Rajneesh Times*, puts it, the ego or personality,

> gets in the way and prevents the individual from discovering and living in another dimension where there is nothing between him and life; a dimension where on the one hand he is open and receptive and happy, and where on the other hand—as an inevitable by-product of being open—he is also willing to feel all that he is, including fears and sorrows, greed and hunger, jealousy and anger, the darkness as well as the light. [18]

The mind-ego blocks our contact with that experience of wholeness which is life itself. Indeed, we are so conditioned, so mind-reactive, so dominated by what the ego tells us to do and experience, that we have no apparent inkling of this experience itself. Which is why Bhagwan has said,

> Ordinarily, you think you are perfectly awake;
> That's a misconception.
> You are completely asleep.
> I can hear you snoring right now;
> You are fast asleep. [19]

The mind ensures that we live in a fog of illusion. Always wanting to discriminate, differentiate, and use words, it cannot recognize the wholeness which lies within. The mind has to go, or at least lose its hold, both because of what it does (playing out unreal and superficial survival strategies) and because of what it prevents (true feelings, an experience of the process of life itself). With the mind in control, only a few will concede that God exists within. Even so, this insight, says Bhagwan, will be purely intellectual. We are duped without knowing it; without knowing that we are already Buddhas. We listen to the interminable voice in our heads and are lulled into the false notion that it is *we* who speak.

How then is mental slavery to be terminated? How are we to come to experience our godliness? In short, how can change be initiated?

It certainly cannot be initiated by the ego. This is bewildering to most of us, given that we are captivated by the ego, the doer, and so are naturally inclined to think in terms of ego-inspired solutions. But solutions of this variety—such as adopting a new moral position or religious creed—serve only to reinforce the hold of the ego. Our core remains untouched:

> A practised virtue is just on the outside, painted.
> You may have practised it so hard
> that it has created a crust around you,
> but deep down you remain the same. [20]

The attempt to change our external circumstances, the social conventions which bind us, is also doomed to failure. Bhagwan is emphatic on this point, saying,

> A revolutionary is one
> who wants to change society,
> who wants to change the government,
> who wants to change the structure—
> economic, political, religious.
> A revolutionary is not spiritual.
> He is not concerned with his own change.
> He thinks that if others change
> then everything will be perfectly okay.
> A revolutionary lives in illusion. [21]

The revolutionary remains untransformed. At best he only succeeds in replacing one set of constraints with another and dupes himself into believing that all has been set to rights. Instead of pursuing red herrings, says Bhagwan, we should simply give up trying to change. Attachment to change is not on, given that Buddhahood is the negation of *all* attachment, a desireless state:

> You are perfect! Nothing else is needed.
> But the mind will say, sooner or later,
> to be something else, to be somewhere else, to become. [22]

It is not even any good making an effort not to change. For if we follow our normal path, following habitual patterns, we end up creating new conflicts: 'If I say to you "Just relax" it is impossible because you do not know what to do. The whole inner turmoil remains . . . and now a new conflict is there: to relax.' [23] True negation of all attachments must clearly involve accepting everything as it is. This alone can free us to experience our totality. However, the fact remains that authentic responses to life can never come from the ego. So something has to change at the ego level. How can this occur if we should not try to change?

Bhagwan's answer is that those of us who want to realize our Buddhahood must begin by recognizing that the secret lies in letting ourselves go:

> A let-go is a let-go!
> Now you don't have any idea what should happen.
> If the past rushes in its rushes in.
> If the future rushes in it comes in.
> You are not even worried about being in the present,
> because that will not allow you to be in a let-go. [24]

To help us, he suggests that we put ourselves in the hands of a Master, a Master who can employ various devices which lift our barriers and so allow enlightenment. He works on what we have closed: 'You cannot bring the divine, but you can hinder its coming. You cannot bring the sun into the house, but you can close the door.' [25] These devices, it should be noted, do not cause change to come about by adding anything new. Instead 'change' is a natural consequence of the ego being dislodged from its pedestal.

Bhagwan suggests that religious seekers should place themselves under the guidance of someone who has already arrived; someone who can then help them to 'lose their minds'. He says that to attempt this goal without a Master is positively dangerous. At one and the same time the mind is our 'illness' and our 'normalcy'. [26] Madness lies ahead if we clumsily dislodge our everyday guide.

The first surrender occurs when seekers stop trying on their own. With initiation they surrender *to* the wisdom and techniques of their Master. These techniques then trigger the crucial surrender, namely surrender *of* the ego. Whatever the surrender, it has to be total:

> If you surrender partially, you are not surrendering. Surrender is always total. And the moment you surrender totally things begin to change. Now you cannot go back to your dreamlife. [27]

In actual practice, both series of surrender go hand in hand, the surrendering of the ego being bound up with surrendering to the Master's path. As Joshi puts it,

> Surrender is not dropping out or giving up one's responsibility; rather

it is abandoning one's old beliefs and values and going on a new adventure by surrendering to the vision of life given by an enlightened master who has transcended the ego. [28]

'Surrender' is central to Rajneeshism. For those taking their first steps on the path it means acknowledging that they are asleep, and trusting Bhagwan. Subsequently, it means using every moment as an opportunity to relinquish everything that prevents them from fully experiencing life. Bhagwan forcefully states,

> Surrender to the divine, to anything—even to a tree—because the real thing is not to whom you surrender: the real thing is the surrendering. Surrender to a tree and the tree will become a teacher to you. Surrender to a stone and the stone will become a god. [29]

Surrender, in other words, is the way to reach that which is alien to the mind but which is man's birthright. It involves giving up past and future in order to concentrate on the present with total awareness. By surrendering to a tree you surrender your ego and so surrender to the divine.

Surrender of this fully fledged variety, which is actually meditation, does not come easily. The ego has first to be prised from its hold. A number of techniques, devices, rituals, are employed to this end. By way of introduction, for these are discussed later in the book, we now mention the more important.

The initiation ritual, 'taking sannyas', sets the context. Says Bhagwan:

> The moment you are a sannyasin you are totally at freedom. It means you have taken a decision and this is the last decision: to live in indecision, to live in freedom. The moment you are initiated into sannyas you are initiated into an uncharted, unplanned future. Now you are not tethered to the past. [30]

The simple ceremony (during which initiates receive a new name, a necklace called a mala, and are told to carry on wearing orange clothes and meditating) highlights the fact that initiates have moved into a new stage of their lives. The new name, the mala, and the clothes do not in themselves help the initiate. Their role is to act as pointers to the inner realm. They are ways of reminding initiates of their relationship with their Master and of their pledge to surrender to the life represented by that relationship.

Taking sannyas points initiates on the way. Meditations which are practised by sannyasins go further. They are designed to help them

Teaching Rajneeshpuram.

throw out their 'madness' and experience themselves in an unfettered state. As Bhagwan says of Dynamic Meditation, which emphasizes catharsis:

> Within moments you can be unburdened of the whole life—of lives even. If you are ready to throw everything, if you can allow your madness to come out, within moments there is a deep cleansing. Now you are cleansed, fresh, innocent. You are a child again. [31]

Then there are the groups. Whether it be primal therapy, encounter, or the Enlightenment Intensives (and the list goes on much longer), the majority of the therapies are seen as powerful ways of exorcising the tyrannical hold of the mind. They are seen as ways of making the participants conscious of formerly unconscious behaviour. This coming to consciousness is what takes the sting out of the mind.

The key term here is 'witnessing', an activity intermediate between mind domination and free-flowing awareness:

> If you begin to be conscious you achieve witnessing. If you begin to be conscious of your acts, conscious of your day-to-day surroundings, conscious of everything that surrounds you, then you begin to witness. [32]

In witnessing there is still the ego (as there has to be, given that there is still something which acts as a witness), but there is no longer attachment to what is being watched. Whatever happens in the emotional and mental realm is simply observed. The therapies and meditations provide settings in which people are encouraged to uncover repressed emotions, emotions which are accepted as neither right nor wrong. By becoming conscious of whatever is going on, by letting things happen in their entirety, and by being non-evaluative, mental states lose their hold. They naturally 'drop off'. Acceptance takes the place of ego-boosting feelings and judgements.

Witnessing, it is held, is a meditative state of being which reduces the mind to its rightful position as servant instead of master. Individuals are then free to express themselves more fully, with much greater acceptance of what is going on. They are no longer victims of their mental states:

> A sannyasin is just like the sky: he lives in the world—hunger comes and satiety; summer comes and winter; good days, bad days; good moods, very elated, ecstatic, euphoric; bad moods, depressed, in the valley, dark, burdened—everything comes and goes and he remains a watcher. [33]

Witnessing is probably the best term to describe how sannyasins live their lives. Witnessing is 'the jumping point from where the jump into awareness becomes possible.[34] Witnessing is not the same as being in a state of permanent free-flowing awareness. In other words, sannyasins are not living the lives of fully enlightened beings—which is why Bhagwan has never defined sannyasins as enlightened.

This is not to say, however, that sannyasins do not want to live permanently in the realm of the unconditioned. They are on the path of moving from the periphery of their being to their centre, their essence, their Buddhahood. The end point is a state of total awareness, ego-lessness, non-duality:

> Awareness means that the total mind has become aware. Now the old mind is not there, but there is a quality of being conscious. Awareness has become the totality; the mind, itself, is now part of the awareness. We cannot say that the mind is aware. We can only meaningfully say that the mind is conscious. Awareness means transcendence of the mind, so it is not the mind that is aware. It is only through transcendence of the mind, through going beyond mind, that awareness is possible. Consciousness is a quality of the mind; awareness is the transcendence. It is going beyond the mind.[35]

In summary, surrender and the enhancement of consciousness are the key ingredients of Bhagwan's path. Techniques of transformation are employed which allow participants both to become aware and to accept what is the case in the face of the mind's exertions to prevent progress.

It remains to say something about how Bhagwan envisages the nature of those who have progressed along his path and their role in the future of mankind. Talk is of the 'new man', basically of the person who can unify all that is good in human and spiritual life. Bhagwan teaches that the salvation of the world rests in the hands of his sannyasins. This is what he has in 'mind' when he writes, 'This century is going to see either the death of all humanity or the birth of a new human being.'[36]

Left to its own devices mankind is teetering on the edge of disaster. Unless humanity is transformed at the level of consciousness, and so in terms of behaviour, we are doomed to extinction. The workings of the ego ensure that we will not survive the current critical phase of our evolution. In particular, we are threatened by a nuclear holocaust. Politicians, regarded by Bhagwan as 'ill people' playing a 'game of lies',[37] will inevitably create strife. The workings of their egos ensure that they are attached to what they have got and will attack anything that threatens them. AIDS, natural disasters, social unrest, and general psychological turmoil reflect the progressive collapse of the current order and mankind's inability to live in harmony with itself and the world.

It is in response to this perilous situation that Bhagwan is implementing his world-transformative vision of the new man. It is only when the world is populated with those who have decided to 'live to the utmost, to the optimum, to the maximum' that a future is possible.[38] Bhagwan's new man must therefore be seen as a salvational response to an apocalyptic millenarian prophecy.

The new man does not reject any of the positive human capacities. The following two extracts from Bhagwan's *Philosophia Perennis* show this clearly:

> The new man will be a mystic, a poet, a scientist, all together. He will not look at life through old, rotten divisions. He will be a mystic because he will feel the presence of God. He will be a poet because he will celebrate the presence of God. And he will be a scientist because he will search into this presence through scientific technology. When a man is all these three things together, the man is whole.
>
> My effort is to create a man who is not partial, who is total, whole, holy. A man should be all these three things together. He should be as accurate and objective as a scientist. He should be as sensitive, as full of heart, as the poet. And he should be rooted deep down in his being as the mystic. He should not choose. He should allow all these dimensions to exist together. And the future belongs to this New Man.[39]

Attachment to the ego, or mind, might be disastrous, but mental faculties must be put to use. The new man must incorporate science.

> I am all for science and technology. The outer world can be transformed totally. We can bring an even better ecological balance than nature itself. Man is nature's highest peak. It is through man that nature can resettle its own problems.[40]

As we have already seen, the mind has to be dislodged from its pedestal. Yet it also has to be used. Bhagwan does not think that this is contradictory. He says, 'My basic fundamental work is to help you to be free of the mind so that you can use it. And if you are the Master, you cannot abuse it; that is impossible.'[41]

Mention of science and technology leads on to other ways in which the new man responds to the challenges of securing the material means to celebrate life. In line with his world-affirming bent, Bhagwan states, 'I don't condemn wealth, wealth is a perfect means which can enhance people in every way, and make their life rich in all. I am a materialist spiritualist.'[42] He says 'blessed are the rich because they are already inheriting the kingdom of God'.[43] Given this, and given his emphasis on freedom, it is no surprise to find that he has always (and consistently) supported the capitalist enterprise. Seen as 'a natural growth',[44] giving people the freedom to be themselves, capitalism is the path to follow—albeit in a different way to how it is normally envisaged.

The new man works hard. Work, though, is not simply a chore to be done to obtain money. What it is to work is transformed. Work becomes 'worship'. Thinking of what worship means in the Christian context, the reader might well be puzzled. How can working, whether it be peeling carrots or applying advanced technology, be an act of worship, particularly when there is no external God to revere? The word is in fact being used in a different sense. As Bhagwan puts it,

> Real worship consists of living.
> Real worship consists of small things.
> Cleaning the floor, and there is worship.
> Worship is a quality — it has nothing to
> do with the act itself, it is the attitude
> you bring to the act. Recognise! See!
> And there is worship.[45]

Work as worship, in other words, is a meditation. It is a way of concentrating on what is happening rather than allowing the mind to engage in its games. It is a way of bringing consciousness to action, thereby 'transforming doing into creativity'.[46] Done with awareness and grounded in love, work becomes a celebration, a way of attuning the self to the 'dance of human energy'.[47]

Embracing capitalist enterprise, the new man can appear to be simply accepting much of life in the West. This apparent theme of acceptance is further enhanced when we bear in mind Bhagwan's assertion that the new man should not renounce the world. He holds that the traditional Indian idea of the sannyasin, giving up material possessions (not to speak of family) in order to devote attention to the struggle for enlightenment, is meaningless. For Bhagwan, spiritual progress should take place in *this* world. However, the new man should not be 'of' the world. The 'content' of his activities might often appear similar to those dominating the lives of non-sannyasins; but, as we have seen with work, his consciousness of them is different. The new man enjoys the richness of experience offered by the world and worldly activities, but only by being unattached to their ego-inspired consequences. What has to be renounced, in other words, are the ways in which worldly activities can generate pride, competitiveness, jealousy, greed, and so on.

What matters to the new man, we have been stressing, is living in the world whilst giving up ego-attachments. Other kinds of renunciation, as with the Indian sannyasins, are fruitless. The new man is not world-rejecting. He experiences the spiritual within the material. This said, it should be pointed out that Bhagwan advocates that a number of important domains of everyday life have to be rejected. They are too ego-inspired and divorced from Buddhahood to be of any value whatsoever.

Organized religions, worldly politics, and traditional notions to do with relationships, sex, marriage, and children are amongst the things rejected. The crucial point is that all these activities are seen as being damned by virtue of their being dominated by externally imposed rules, stereotypes, and expectations. Consider traditional marriage. Bhagwan rejects the idea of marriage as a partnership entered into for life, functioning as an end in itself in that partners continually strive to live in terms of the ideal. Bhagwan rejects marriage as a stereotyped 'ought'. Instead, marriage is seen as an expression of authenticity. To get trapped in marriage, to get obsessed with issues of fidelity, providing a home for children and so on, is to lose contact with what really matters, the immediacy of true feeling. This is why Bhagwan writes:

> Marriage is only a working partnership. If it works, good. If it does not work, then say goodbye. I don't think it's anything sacred. It is just an instrument and a working partnership; nothing to be bothered about so much. [48]

At least marriage is not entirely dismissed. Other traditional institutions do not fare so well. As already indicated, Bhagwan is entirely disparaging of traditional politics. For him political change, in particular transcending divisional boundaries to do with race, nationality, and so on, has to do with the transformation of consciousness. Politicians are so wrapped up in their attachments that they can only argue for what they believe to be right. They are responsible to their ideologies, not to the values of Buddhahood.

Much the same can be said of traditional religions. These do not cater for anything other than the demands of the ego. Bhagwan puts it graphically:

> Christianity, Hinduism, Judaism,
> Churches, Mosques, Temples,
> organised around a creed,
> organised because of the fear of men,
> organised because of the mind escaping
> from inner emptiness.
> Doctrines, dogmas to fill you.
> These are all barriers. [49]

It should be apparent by now that Bhagwan's new man combines the themes of rejecting whatever stands in the way of transformation and accepting that which can be put to the service of spiritual growth. Putting it simply, on the one hand traditional religion is rejected; on the other capitalism is incorporated. Responses to mainstream institutions are gauged in terms of the basic characteristics of the new man. These characteristics are summarized by Bhagwan in the following terms. The new man,

> is open and honest. He is transparently real, authentic and self-disclosing. He will not be a hypocrite. He will not live through goals: he will live here now. He will only know one time, now, and only one space, here. And through that presence he will know what God is. [50]

Anything which leads to living in terms of external codes must go. Only then can the new man live in terms of his natural, spontaneous virtues.

> The new man will live not through ideologies, not through moralities, but through consciousness. The new man will live through awareness. The new man will be responsible to himself and to existence. The new man will not be moral in the old sense; he will be amoral. [51]

It should be explained, however, that talk of amorality, talk along the lines that 'anything is okay providing you don't get too attached to it', should not imply that the new man is just as inclined to do bad as to do good. The new man is informed by his Buddhahood.

There is much more to be said about the new man, epitomizing as he does the nature of Bhagwan's teaching. Many of these additional characterizations, such as those to do with emotional life, are looked at later. We conclude this chapter by summarizing the main features.

The single most important thing is that the new man provides 'a new way of being in the cosmos, a qualitatively different way of perceiving and experiencing reality'. [52] This provides a way of avoiding the traps which traditional forms of life generate. To the extent that mind is 'gone', so have greed, ambition, competition, traditional religion, traditionally envisaged relationships and so on. All these 'exist in the mind'. [53] At the same time, though, the new man unifies 'life in its totality'. He combines science (which leads to 'richness on the outside') and religion (which leads to 'richness in your innermost core'). He combines the qualities of Zorba the Greek and Gautama the Buddha (he is Zorba the Buddha, a life-affirming, celebratory, yet meditative person). Unifying these characteristics, and others such as femininity and masculinity, the new man is no longer a battleground of divergent ways of being. He provides *the* way of circumventing all the tensions, strains, disruptions, and divisions which are currently leading mankind to disaster.

In the next chapter we discuss the specific techniques designed to create the new man. In a later chapter we look at how the new man lives in communes, or Buddhafields. The new man is not simply a utopian ideal. Bhagwan has taken a number of practical steps to implement his vision. The 'Buddhafields' provide an instance. The problem of AIDS, it will be recalled, has been addressed. So too has the question of over-population. Since 1981 sannyasins have virtually ceased to bear children. And whatever the role of military-styled organizations during the recent years at Rajneeshpuram, it seems incontestable that sannyasins are generally a peace-loving people.

3
Techniques of Transformation: 'Waking the Buddhas'

Everything Bhagwan does, everything that
happens around him is a technique. He
pokes us, prods us, seduces us into
transformation.

Ma Satya Bharti

As we have seen, we are all 'gods and goddesses in exile', condemned
to remain at the periphery of our being until our 'garbage' has been
put into place.

Bhagwan calls himself a 'Master of Masters'. [1] Claiming to possess
the spiritual insight to see what is holding people back from their
authentic being, he is able to provide techniques for his disciples.
Their ultimate purpose is to awaken a state of meditative awareness.

The techniques are drawn from a wide range of sources, and
Rajneesh practices often combine components from different
traditions. Sufism is fused with Freudian techniques; yogic breathing
runs alonside Tibetan practices; eastern and western practices meet
and intermingle—Taoist, Buddhist, Jain, Hindu, Hassidic, Jungian,
Reichian and humanistic.

The techniques are also numerous. Likening Bhagwan to a surgeon,
whose job it is to cut through all the garbage 'with a deft precision',
Bharti writes that 'he does it with a thousand tricks, not the least
of which is laughter.' [2] Bhagwan himself explains why he has
assembled such a diverse package by saying:

> I have to provoke so many different types of minds, different types
> of sleeps are there. I ring a bell: it may help somebody to wake up,
> to somebody else it may look like a lullaby. He will need something
> else—maybe a hit on the head, or cold water thrown on him, or a
> good shaking. Different people need different approaches to be
> provoked. [3]

With so many techniques, Bhagwan ensures that whatever the needs and conditions of his sannyasins there are appropriate remedies and devices available to them. Those living in his communes, those visiting his centres, those who have recently joined the movement, those sannyasins who are happy to remain living in the outside world—all tend to be directed to and affected by different techniques. Few, if any, of the particular techniques discussed in the following pages are practised by all sannyasins.

In Poona days, visitors to the ashram (whether sannyasins or not) would normally participate in group therapies and formal meditations. Group therapies on offer included encounter, neo-Reichian bodywork, polarity balancing, primal therapy, hypnotherapy, bio-energetics, the Samarpan group, the Awareness group, the Anatta group, Enlightenment Intensive, the Centreing group, the Leela group, and the Tantra group. Formal meditations included the famous Dynamic Meditation, and the Kundalini, Nadabrahma, and Gourishankar meditations. Therapies were put on for two weeks in every four. Meditation camps ran from the eleventh to the twentieth of every month, five different meditations being performed daily. Therapies cost up to 1000 rupees each. A one-hundred rupee book of tickets sufficed for the ten days of the camps.

The therapies and formal meditations often brought about a sense of an experiential connection with Bhagwan in those who were to become sannyasins, or revitalized an already existing sense of awareness. Worshippers, namely those sannyasins who worked in the ashram, had already participated in either therapies or formal meditations. Having finished their involvement with these techniques, their work was a technique instead. It was a meditation for them, a worship, and the environment of the commune was adjudged to be as efficient as any group or formal meditation in unmasking the ego. The confrontative and unsettling nature of life in the commune was seen to be particularly important in this respect.

In Rajneeshism, then, techniques of transformation cover a wide range: Bhagwan's laughter, eastern meditations, work, Freudian therapies, and, we might add, the sheer presence of Bhagwan himself. For the present, however, we concentrate on group therapies and formal meditations; on the powerful techniques which are usually the first to make a significant impact on the tyrannical hold of the mind.

Sally Belfrage describes how a friend of hers, a novice sannyasin, arrived at Poona and was 'plunged instantly into a "primal therapy group"—two weeks to shake his world.'[4] Using catharsis to get in touch with repressed and painful emotions of a 'primal' nature, Belfrage's friend Devopama realized the extent to which his normal 'world' was a precarious artefact. He also learnt much more about himself, his 'insanity', his fears.

Of the therapies, however, Teertha's[5] Encounter groups had the reputation of being among the best and certainly among the toughest. Each ran for seven days. Under the guidance of Teertha, 'the angelic Rasputin',[6] participants confronted each other, confronted themselves, acted out fantasies and guilts, fought, made love, catharted, sulked, resisted, and surrendered. The emphasis was very much on spontaneous action rather than on carefully thought out and verbalized interchange. Thus Teertha began each group with the injunction, 'The way to do work in this group is to do it. Not to talk about it, but to do it.'[7]

The freedom of expression provided by the closed environment allowed participants to look at their 'trips'; to look at the behaviour patterns of the ego. Faced with others who were perfectly prepared to be open and critical, individuals found that they could no longer get away with or hide behind their customary strategies for survival. These attacks on barriers were sometimes quite naturally experienced as frightening and could give rise to violent emotion:

> For the first day and a half of the group, Moksha was paralyzed with fear. He sat along the wall, hoping no-one would notice him, that no-one would confront him. But of course they had, they did. They'd try to provoke him, try to press his buttons, but he'd refused to fight. Everyone else in the room would be fighting, but he'd sit on the outside watching. Crying, frightened . . . He was violent in his non-violence. He saw his anger, he recognized it for what it was. He was afraid of it.
>
> It was the afternoon of the second day. 'You hate me' he screamed, pointing his finger at someone, not even knowing who it was. 'You hate me. I know it. I can feel it.' The barrier was broken.
>
> He was more frightened than ever.
>
> 'Pound the wall' Teertha told him, 'Let it all out.'
>
> 'Go over to every person in the group' Teertha told him finally, 'and tell them what you think of them. Kill them with your words.'
>
> Moksha went over to Deva. Suddenly his hands were around her neck.
>
> Teertha's voice in his ear. Soft, insistent:
> 'Surrender surrender . . .'
> But he didn't want to surrender. He wanted to kill.

People were pushed to their limits, indeed well beyond the limits of how they would normally behave. Breakthrough could then occur. Moksha, we have seen, 'wanted to kill'. 'Surrender' said Teertha,

> And it happened. He felt himself going inward, disappearing—a circle, becoming smaller and smaller. He lost his sense of balance, fell to the ground. All the energy that had been rushing outward was suddenly inside him. It exploded out of the top of his head.
> Nothingness.
> No thoughts, no mind, no ego, no self.
> An empty space. Moksha ceased to exist, he became one with the whole. [8]

It is perhaps necessary to say that no one ever died during groups. But they were felt to go much further than their Western counterparts in pushing people into confrontation and new experiences.

A group of a rather different ilk at Poona was the Enlightenment Intensive. This highly organized three or seven day group included a number of formal meditation techniques which are discussed later in the chapter. Basically it was a group therapy characterized by concentrated attention on questioning habitual responses. The tightly structured nature of the daily routine can be seen in the schedule:

6.00 – 7.00	Dynamic Meditation
7.00 – 9.30	sessions
9.30 – 10.00	breakfast
10.00 – 11.30	sessions
11.30 – 12.00	walk
12.00 – 13.00	sessions
13.00 – 15.00	lunch, wash, sleep
15.00 – 16.00	sessions
16.00 – 16.30	walk
16.30 – 17.30	sessions
17.30 – 18.30	Kundalini Meditation
18.30 – 19.30	sessions
19.30 – 20.00	supper
20.00 – 21.00	silent meditation
21.00 – 22.00	sessions
22.00 – 22.30	body exercises
22.30 – 23.30	sessions [9]

During the eight daily 'sessions' participants paired up. One person would ask the other: 'Tell me who you are?' The other would then have five minutes in which to respond, during which time the questioner should remain as impassive as possible. Participants were not allowed to communicate with others outside the group. Their attention had to remain concentrated on the 'koan' 'Who am I?' (When this question was answered, others would be set by the group leader.)

One sannyasin has described it as a group in which participants are forced to stay with themselves, to look at themselves, to become conscious of all their identities and roles. Participants come to realize the extent to which their egos put up defences when ego-identity is threatened. Most participants experience boredom, sleepiness, itchiness, aches and pains—all seen as ways used by the ego to resist the recognition that its identity is being questioned. Who can remain satisfied with such responses as 'I am a mother' on being continually asked 'Who are you?'

The group is about getting beyond ego-identities and their consequences. Simant told us that she came to experience a sense of being which she had had glimpses of in the past, but which had been lost with the passing years and the bustle of daily life:

I did Enlightenment Intensive, the 'Who am I' group, and everything just changed. I really can't begin to describe everything that happened for me in that group except that on the second day, in the afternoon, I suddenly realized something which had been my heart's desire since I was about eleven, that I had totally given up on by the time I was about fifteen, the understanding that everything was one. I was a very intellectual kid and it was obvious logically and in every way that everything was one, but I had the intense yearning to experience it. When I had given up on this dream I had put all my energy into the social aspect of it, to community, harmony and people working together. I had forgotten the spiritual side that this had come from. Then in the group I had the startling experience of having no edge to myself, suddenly realizing I couldn't feel any boundary between me and the rest of the world. This thing I had come to know as ME was actually totally connected. That was it, this thing I had yearned for so long, but it wasn't just an intellectual belief for those few minutes . . . At whatever level was possible for me that day I knew what Bhagwan was offering.

A former sannyasin draws attention to how the group allowed him to go beyond the last defences of his ego:

You must face yourself, all your thoughts, feelings, fears, all alone—

and you start to see how unimportant you are, how little all this that you are talking about does matter. My own experience was that on the third day I started to cry and vomit; I couldn't face myself any more, I got sick—the group leader then told me to sit down in front of a mirror and look at myself. Vomiting and crying I then experienced myself as a nothing, I could see through myself, see what was behind; something much greater, lighter, purer than I, my ego, ever could be, something which was divine. It was like throwing everything out of myself, psychologically as well as physically, and reaching the pure centre of emptiness—enlightenment. [10]

Another sannyasin tells of how his Enlightenment Intensive group brought him to appreciate that the art of going beyond the ego is to accept whatever the moment holds. The ego makes judgements, in this case that 'being stuck' is a bad state to be in. Accepting 'stuckness', Neeraj moved beyond:

> In it I touched the surface of where Bhagwan is all the time. I answered the first question 'Who am I' after four days and the second question I was given by the group leader was 'How is life fulfilled?'. On the sixth day I rationalized this into an answer that sounded pretty good and so said to the group leader, 'The answer is that life is fulfilled if you are totally conscious.'
> She said, 'And what if you are not totally conscious?'
> 'Then life isn't fulfilled', I replied.
> I realized at that point that I was as far away as ever.
> She then gave me these questions.
> 'How is life fulfilled for a battered child?'
> 'How is life fulfilled for a drunk?'
> 'How is life fulfilled for a person in a concentration camp?'
> The more I asked these questions, the more blocked I felt. So, after struggling for hours, I said to the group leader that I was completely stuck, to which she said,
> 'How is life fulfilled by being stuck?'
> That night I didn't sleep. The question was with me all the time. In the early morning the answer suddenly hit me. My whole being knew. We had been told to go for a walk before starting the last day of the group, so I got up and life was just beginning. I walked down to the river and it was like seeing it for the first time. I was very, very present. Smelling, touching, tasting—every sensation was a new experience. That was an immense experience for me. For Bhagwan it is like that all the time. Everything is constantly new. Even now when I'm feeling blocked I ask myself that question and come back to the present. It was then that I understood fully what being a sannyasin really meant.

Not all the groups in Poona were quite so intensive. The Centreing group involved concentration on exercises aimed at 'emptying the mind'. Nevertheless, these games were seen as amusing and fun to do. One exercise, for example, involved repeating 'a very difficult rhyme of absolutely senseless words—you do this in couples, walking around in the Mahatma Gandhi road in Poona.[11]

Other groups included such activities as guided fantasy (to probe the unconscious), bio-energetics (using physical stress positions to release bodily-mental blocks), breathing exercises (to shake up habitual suppressive strategies), catharsis (to release repressed emotions), dancing (to loosen inhibition and heighten energy), and role playing (to lose identity attachment and see unconscious patterns). What though of sex? After all, Poona had an infamous reputation for sexual promiscuity.

This reputation was not entirely undeserved. Sally Belfrage, on leaving the ashram, was asked 'But didn't you get laid?' She replied 'Eh?' Her interrogator continued, 'Well for God's sake, baby, what do you think the groups are for? You mean to tell me you haven't got laid? At all?[12] One group in particular revolved around sex. The Tantra group was an exploration of sexual conditioning, of taboos and blocks. Members articulated hitherto hidden sexual fears and problems, and were encouraged to talk about them frankly in order to free themselves from their constraints. But they were also encouraged to fully express their sexuality as well, without the normal interference of mind or moral judgement:

> Suddha turned off the lights in the room and turned on loud, earthy rock music.
>
> 'Feel the animal inside you' she told them. It was a technique she used often in the group. 'Everyone has an animal inside them. Allow yourself to feel it.' They began slowly, awkwardly, hesitantly, making animal sounds, animal gestures. After a few minutes Suddha told them 'Now begin to express it. Move around. Be total. Let anything happen, no matter how freaky it gets.'
>
> They began interacting with each other: playful, frisky animals, fighting, loving, rolling on the ground, rolling on top of each other. 'Be more total! Get into it more!' Suddha yelled from time to time. After a while they began to lose all sense of who they were, where they were, their past, their conditionings. It was as if another reality had descended on the room, as if they were tripping on acid, living out their suppressed desires, their fantasies, with no inhibitions.
>
> There was no goal to it, there was nothing that had to happen, so they could play with it, play with their sexuality. Krishna could

be loving to someone one minute, playing with them, caressing them, and the next minute, if she felt like it, she could simply leave, without feeling guilty about it. If she wanted to move into sex with someone she could; if she didn't want to, she didn't have to. No promises were made, no expectations had to be disappointed. There could be feelings of love without sex and sexuality without love. She made love to a small oriental man, not her type at all. A pure energy phenomenon. They moved from one intricate position to another, like a ballet choreographed by God. The lovemaking went on and on, there was no end to it. Who he was, who she was, didn't matter. Their personalities, their egos, had nothing to do with it. Neither was exploiting the other; they were both giving, loving, sharing. They fell asleep finally in each other's arms. When they got up from their sleep, whatever energy existed between them was gone. They were just two people in the group. There was no shyness between them, no mind-induced sense of connection, no avoiding the other or lusting for the other. They had shared something beautiful, something pure. Now it no longer existed. There were no strings attached, no commitments. A gift. [13]

The group therapies, it will be seen, are powerful, working in various ways to trigger various experiences. A recent article in *The Rajneesh Times* [14] helps unravel the complicated story of what is going on by drawing attention to what the therapies have in common. 'Rajneesh Spiritual Therapy', as the approach is called in the article, is described as 'humanistic psychotherapy that has been transformed'. Humanistic activities (whether they be encounter, gestalt, bio-energetics, psychosynthesis, primal screaming, rebirthing, and so on) have been transformed by virtue of their 'being in the hands of an Enlightened Master'. Although Bhagwan does not actually run groups, his 'spiritual therapists' function as vehicles for his transformative presence: 'the way they conduct their programs has its source in the meditative space within themselves, that has opened up through being with Him'. The meditative space, provided by Bhagwan, adds a 'context' which goes beyond anything found in the humanistic realm. The context is of 'love, awareness, freedom, celebration, live-affirmation, creativity, relevance, responsibility, truth, and commitment—all unconditional!'

Spiritual therapists work to effect a 'quantum leap into Bhagwan's enlightened context'; they work to effect a 'shift from a content-oriented way of living to a context-oriented way'. Bhagwan's context means that the therapists have little or no interest in working at the level of content. Their own detachment from ego (which is where content lies) ensures that they have no inclination to struggle 'through the mountains of junk that constitute people's personalities and problems'; they ignore the interminable 'noise and fog of personality'; they have no interest in helping provide solutions to questions of the 'do I want a divorce?' variety; they are not concerned with patching up people's egos. Not being clogged up with these concerns, the spiritual therapists are able to work at a much more profound level:

> It is precisely because they do not get drawn into working on the computer-like content of people's minds that they have as much room as they have to really *be* with the people who come to them.

Participants, their content or garbage more or less ignored, respond to their experiences of the therapist. They 'find themselves tuning into where the therapist is—disengaging from the content in order to find the same space within themselves'. Participants are able to respond to the 'spark of life' which already exists within:

> When all the attention being paid to it (content) is released, an abundance of free-flowing energy becomes available. It is this suddenly available energy that precipitates people into awareness of their inner being, that opens the doors of the feeling and the heart, that turns the little spark of life into a vibrant flame, and that is the source of—and means to—celebrating life rather than merely surviving.

The job of the therapist, then, is to 'awaken, nourish and celebrate the life within the participants'. Participants come to shift from 'endlessly working on what could be, or should be, or was' to 'living in conscious, loving and joyful contact with what really is'.

Rajneesh Spiritual Therapy, it is apparent, is heavily dependent on the 'presence' of Bhagwan. It relies on 'His context'. Ultimately, therapy is in the hands of God:

> 'A therapist doesn't have to do anything' Bhagwan says, 'He just has to become a vehicle for God's energy. He has to become like a hollow bamboo so that God can work through him; he has to become a passage.'[15]

The importance of Bhagwan-God is also seen in the fact that participants generally feel secure enough to go further than they have ever gone before. Karuna, for example,

> found that I could go beyond the point where I had always gotten stuck before when I was in groups. Bhagwan was there giving me

the permission to go ahead, to transcend all boundaries. [16]

Bhagwan's presence somehow diminishes the fears of those taking group therapies; their fears of insanity, total loss of individuality, of 'no return', and so on. Bhagwan himself accepts that 'without a Master you will go mad'. [17] But most participants feel that they are in the hands of a Master, a Master they can trust.

There is more to the dynamics of the group therapies than the role played by the presence of Bhagwan. We have to consider Bhagwan's understanding of 'energy'. But before turning to this it is useful to look at the formal meditations. Unlike the group therapies these techniques are done alone. Meditators might come together, but there is little interaction, and certainly none of a confrontational kind. Otherwise, however, therapies and meditations share many of the same basic dynamics.

Dynamic Meditation is the best known of the formal meditations. The majority of the other meditations (and there are over a hundred in all) draw upon at least one aspect of this basic technique. Dynamic Meditation is split into five distinct stages, each lasting for ten minutes. It is performed with eyes closed, many often blindfolding themselves in order to better concentrate on what is happening to them.

The first stage involves deep, fast breathing through the nose. This breathing should be irregular, chaotic even, in order to disturb the normal patterns of the body. This, says Bhagwan, allows emotional blocks to rise to the surface. Not a few find this breathing difficult. One sannyasin has described it as 'torturous'. She continues,

> I could breathe deeply or I could breathe rapidly, but to do both seemed impossible. Long before the breathing period was over my chest was hurting, my neck was hurting. My whole body was moving with the effort, aching with the effort. *I don't want to do this*, I started saying to myself. *I hate it, I hate it, I can't do it, I just can't.*

Then, 'my breathing took over and "I" wasn't doing it; the breathing was happening by itself.' [18]

Their emotional blocks poised for release, meditators are told to express completely whatever comes up. They have entered the second, cathartic, stage of the sequence. Typically they confront painful emotions: those which have been repressed by society, which have been too distressful for the individuals concerned to come to terms with, or which the meditators have simply felt too inhibited to express. [19]

Vachana tells us she likes the cathartic stage of the Dynamic Meditation because it allows her to escape from her blocks, allows her to open up her heart:

> If I have a lot of stuff on my chest Dynamic Meditation certainly works for me. I have a lot of crying to do, and I can't tell you where it comes from. There's sadness, there's frustration, anger, depression. I've always been up and down, and the thing about Dynamic Meditation is that if I concentrate on the breathing part, when it comes to the next bit I cry an awful lot. It's going deeper into whatever feelings are in the way of enjoying life and being open to others. When I'm blocked my heart feels closed. Stuff will come up again from deep down where it's been suppressed through a need to keep going and be there for other people and all the old conditioning. If I stop being positive and let that gap come then the other side of the picture is there: the fear, the sadness or whatever it's about.

Divya did not even know that she had a lot of 'stuff' inside her, at least not anger or loneliness: 'No-one ever told me I was angry, I just discovered it. No-one told me that I needed more love. It became very obvious.' Catharsis has helped her to become aware of what is buried deep within. Dayal makes much the same point in speaking of the catharsis stage: 'Dynamic is the one meditation where it's impossible to hide from yourself the fact that you are avoiding something, some emotion, some memory. It's just horribly obvious.'

Expression and release increase awareness. They also result in a considerable display of energy:

> I lay on the sand; I screamed, I cried. Wetness poured from my eyes, my nose, my mouth. My body jerked and writhed in epileptic-like movements. I vomited, and kicked the sand ferociously to cover the mess I had made. Anger came up. I punched the air, I growled like a lion, I killed my mother and father and the beggar I had seen on the street that morning and a multitude of strangers I'd never met. [20]

The third stage is also energetic. Meditators have to jump up and down shouting, 'hoo, hoo, hoo'. This mantra 'hits' the vital energies of the 'sex centre', triggering their upward flow into the high 'centres' of the body. The energy flow is meant to increase spirituality. Whatever the theory of this, and the subject is returned to in a moment, it is apparent that Dynamic Meditation has now ceased to be psychotherapeutic in nature. The first two stages have parallels in the western psychotherapeutic tradition of healing by releasing emotional and physical blocks. The third stage has to do with transforming sexual energy into spiritual power.

Not that participants invariably experience energy arousal in spiritual terms. Dayananda says,

> I enjoy the third stage, the 'hoo, hoo, hoo', but that's where I get stuck. The first time I felt like throwing up and I didn't know that bins are always provided in Dynamic for this very purpose, so I fought the impulse. I pushed it down, and immediately wanted to have a shit. So I brought the energy up again, only to feel sick. I was oscillating between the two.

After three stages demanding intense and total commitment, meditation happens—'by itself'. The music accompanying the 'hoo, hoo, hoo' abruptly stops and participants stay motionless. One participant from Poona days records,

> My body dropped to the ground, depleted by the effort of the first three stages. It was exhausted, but the energy was still alive inside me, like an electric current, running through me but not me. And in another way feeling more like me, the reality of me, than my body or mind or emotions. Meditation happened. There was no way for it not to happen. Whether I wanted it or not, whether I believed in it or not. Peace. Bliss. That-which-has-no-words. The beyond within. [21]

The meditation ends with participants expressing their thanks and celebrating their experience of Buddhahood.

Kundalini Meditation has been another favourite. It also combines violent activity with passivity. Bhagwan says,

> First let your complete organism be tense, and go on being tense to the optimum, to your fullest possibility. And then suddenly you will feel a relaxation setting in. This awareness is meditation. [22]

For the first fifteen minutes, meditators are told to shake until they 'become' the shaking. Energy is awakened. The next fifteen minutes involves dancing. It allows some dissipation of what could otherwise be a rather disquieting amount of tension. Meditators then remain still and receptive, listening to gentle music. Finally, and in total silence, they are told to lie down and 'just be'.

Kundalini is the energy meditation *par excellence*. Physical energy or tension is held to trigger that spiritual energy which, in accord with Tantric tradition, is held to lie in the lowest of the seven centres of the body. Once aroused this spiritual energy is experienced not as tension but as bliss.

Energy darshan. Poona, 1979.

Another favourite meditation, the Nadabrahma, is less frenetic, although also concerned with energy. Said to be a Tibetan practice, participants hum together for thirty minutes, visualizing their bodies as empty bamboo-like vessels filled only with vibration. Meditators then move their arms in such a way as to transfer their energy outward to the universe. This is followed by arm movements bringing energy back into themselves. Participants then sit absolutely immobile for a further fifteen minutes.

One further meditation worthy of note is the Gourishankar Meditation, involving the Sufi 'latihan' process of automatic movement. Participants lead up to latihan by breathing deeply and slowly (listening to music with a beat seven times as fast as that of a normal heart-rate), their inhalations and exhalations being held as long as possible. Having also stared intently at a flickering light, meditators are told to allow their bodies to move—without any conscious exertion. After this latihan period, perfect stillness follows for fifteen minutes.

Having introduced the reader to some of the techniques it is time to take stock. It is time to explore how Bhagwan understands his therapies and formal meditations to work, their objectives and dynamics.

Most generally, techniques transform sannyasins by allowing movement from the periphery to the centre. As Bharti puts it, 'Psychotherapy leads to meditation. Meditation leads to awareness. Awareness leads to being.'[23] Freeing the self from the ego, techniques nurture a state of consciousness which operates out of an entirely different context from the old. An essential ingredient of the movement from the periphery, we have already seen, is provided by Bhagwan's presence, by his 'context'. But exactly how do the specific techniques contribute to transformation?

'The purpose of therapy', says Bhagwan, 'is to bring you to a point where you can see your unnaturalness.'[24] The same can be said of formal meditations. By becoming aware of what is unnatural sannyasins are transformed. To refer again to Bhagwan,

The natural can exist without your cooperation, but the unnatural cannot exist. Once you have seen that it is unnatural, your grip on it becomes loose. Your fist opens of its own accord.

The group is not a device to open your fist. It is just to help you see that what you are doing is unnatural. In that very seeing, the transformation.[25]

The idea, then, is that the hold of the ego is weakened, and transformation occurs, when sannyasins become aware of their reactive systems. The techniques we have introduced instil awareness by a variety of means. Habitual physical actions are shaken up and highlighted by the chaotic breathing of Dynamic Meditation. Repressed, hidden emotions are brought into consciousness by primal therapy. Encounter groups enable participants to see the games they have been playing. Enlightenment intensives reveal identity commitments. Especially in Poona days these awareness engendering techniques took a radical form. [26] Committed to its survival and repressing things which it does not want to face, the ego is not easily dislodged from its pedestal. This is why sannyasins of those days used to say that 'only by extremes can transformation occur'.

So far so good. Techniques provide awareness. However, things now get rather more complicated. Bhagwan provides apparently different accounts of the ways in which techniques work on what has been brought into consciousness. One strand of his teaching stresses that transformation occurs simply by virtue of sannyasins becoming aware of their reactive systems. Another, more radical, strand stresses that it is not enough to become aware of the 'the unnatural' and be content to live with it. What is unnatural must go.

According to the first of these options transformation occurs when participants become aware that they are 'imprisoned' by their minds. Consciousness of ego-attachments is bound up with a 'letting go' of what *remain* as reactive systems. As Simant told us,

> More and more I became aware that I couldn't stop thinking throughout the meditations, and that everything Bhagwan had been saying in the morning was totally applicable. I couldn't escape my mind. I was a total victim, a slave of my mind. There seemed no way to stop this thinking, chattering ego.

Paradoxically, her awareness of the tyranny of the mind provides her with that freedom and detachment needed for transformation.

Nothing changes other than one's awareness of it. This means an emphasis on accepting everything. As Bhagwan says, 'nothing in God's world is to be denied. You just have to drop your interpretations.' [27] Techniques of transformation are not to do with getting rid of garbage. Forced to face the truth about themselves instead of hiding behind what they want to be sannyasins have to accept 'the darkness as well as the light'. [28] Bharti goes so far as to write, the reader will recall, that:

It's Bhagwan's acceptance of everything—absolutely, uncon-ditionally—that seems to be the one common thread that runs through all his teachings. Accept yourself, accept life, accept things as they are. The Ganges and the sewer water—to Bhagwan, both are equally sacred. He tells us to accept our pains and our frustrations, to accept our non-acceptance.[29]

Instead of getting rid of garbage, techniques are seen as working to 'integrate' followers. Bringing distressful experiences to the surface, consciousness ensures that their hold is weakened, and that they are accepted as being part of what one is. This theme is particularly pronounced in Bhagwan's teaching on the new man. It is seen in the following extract describing the 'Acceptance Group' at Medina:

ACCEPTANCE: The rejection of any aspect of ourselves blocks our ability to feel at ease both with ourselves and others. The way to acceptance lies in our daring to expose those parts we have judged as imperfect and kept hidden from view. The main focus will be on using the group as a mirror in which to see that we don't have to be perfect to be loved.[30]

In contrast to the theme of accepting everything, for good or for bad, Bhagwan also teaches that techniques can affect our garbage. It is not simply that techniques allow participants to see their own unnaturalness: the second strand of Bhagwan's teaching is that the unnatural has to go. It is of course true that the first strand also does away with unnaturalness, on the grounds that awareness renders the unnatural natural. But the fact remains that there is a difference between accepting everything (albeit in a transformed fashion) and discarding what is deemed to be undesirable. There is a contrast between saying to a homosexual 'be authentic, accept yourself' and saying 'it is a disease'.[31]

What is now emphasized is freedom from whatever restricts. Sannyasins should be freed from conditioning, superfluous layers, blocks, dark 'ego-spaces', whatever is illusory, distorted, or repressed; indeed, from all that is ego. Sannyasins should 'let go' of all that prevents the natural occurrence of meditative awareness. They should move through the ego to the God which lies within. As Bharti says, Bhagwan 'helps us to strip away layer after layer of false accumulations. To be with him is to be engaged in a getting-rid-of process.'[32]

So how do techniques work to dispose of garbage? More radically still, how do they facilitate the state of 'no-mind'? Bhagwan claims that 'Anything incomplete is carried by the mind for ever and ever. Anything complete is dropped.' He continues, 'The mind has a tendency to carry incomplete things just in the hope that someday there may be an opportunity to complete them.'[33] Techniques provide the opportunity for finishing things off. This is where catharsis comes in. Contrary to the everyday view that emotional indulgence tends to whet the appetite, Bhagwan teaches that emotional activity results in purgation. In accordance with his Freudian-like view that repressed emotions are especially distortive, catharsis has to go deep. Great importance is attached to the liberating role of emotional expression:

> To teach you how to be free and sane, I'll have to devise all sorts of mad games. Through these mad games, the accumulated madness within you can be acted out, thrown out.
>
> Because the world is mad—because everyone is mad—catharsis is needed. People have to be helped so they can throw their repressions unconditionally. If they want to shriek and shout and scream, they have to be allowed. If they want to weep and cry, they have to be allowed. When a person goes crazy on his own, deliberately, he becomes unburdened.[34]

According to Belfrage, Bhagwan 'finished with sex in his past lives and does not need it anymore'.[35] Sannyasins of Poona days used Tantric-inspired techniques to experience their sexuality totally. Like Bhagwan, their ultimate aim was the freedom of authentic celibacy. Together with catharsis, another important aspect of the aim of moving beyond emotionality and desire is to adopt the stance of 'witness'. Sexual arousal, anger, pretty well any emotional attachment can be dropped by watching it.

The contrast with the first 'acceptance' strand of Bhagwan's teaching is becoming more pronounced. We began with talk of 'accepting darkness' together with 'light'. We moved on to the theme of discarding 'madness'. Our introduction of sex makes it clear that 'madness' involves all ego-inspired experiences, including what we normally think of as being positive. Garbage is widespread. Garbage is, in fact, *anything* which prevents us from living at the centre of our being, as gods. It includes positive-seeming attachments and experiences.

So far we have been concentrating on how therapies and formal meditations work on the ego. But there is another side to the story. Techniques also work in more positive fashion to nurture experiences of what lies within. Buddha consciousness is a natural consequence of freedom from the ego. But there is more to it than this. Techniques work on 'energy'. Dynamic and Kundalini meditations, the Nadabrahma meditation, Tantric groups and so on: all involve the unblocking and moving of spiritual energy. In such a way, the energy lost through the physical exertion of catharsis is often felt to be more than replenished by the resultant liberation of energy that was previously trapped or working against itself because of counter-productive beliefs or repressed emotion. Recall Moksha's response to Teertha's encounter group: all the energy that had been rushing outward was suddenly inside him. And it is this energy which rises through the body to explode; to render Moksha one with the whole. Or, as Bhagwan puts it, 'Meditation is the deepest phenomena happening, the explosion of the life-force. In meditation a living cell—a living being—explodes.' [36]

Bhagwan has had much to say on the subject, including, for example, the nature of energy. (The reader is referred to *Meditation: The Art of Ecstasy* [1976] for further details.) It is impossible to do full justice to how he understands techniques to work, or, for that matter, what they work to do. Another complication is that Bhagwan's teachings on the subject have changed over the years. We have not been able to disentangle the old from the new in this account. Suffice it to say that the shift has been from 'killing the ego' to 'classes in the heart'. A number of the earlier aggressive therapies have been modified. The trend is away from experiencing without the ego to experiencing love at the heart of every being. We conclude with two accounts which capture the development. The first is taken from an ex-sannyasin reflecting on his experiences at Poona. The second is from a 1983 Medina brochure describing the therapies offered by the commune.

> Bhagwan is asocial—he allows everything. He takes you into something, somewhere, where you lose yourself and your grasp of outside reality. This is the problem. It is very hard, almost impossible for a western person to drop his ego, his personality, his grasp on the outside world. For myself, after a few months in Poona, this 'killing my ego' became a regular struggle—a struggle between my old 'I', my sensible, thinking personality, and my new, not-thinking, floating 'being'. I was living in an inner ecstasy where the surroundings did not matter, where I had no will left of my own (or rather a very confused will). [37]

> The whole purpose of the groups is to create an environment in which people can see themselves more clearly, have insights into the reasons

why they behave as they do, and see how the behaviour they exhibit is often stopping them from receiving the love and nourishment from those around them. The emotionally mature, emotionally full person is someone who is able to participate fully in life. We're aiming at a maturity and balance in life. [38]

4
The Quality of Life: 'Coming Closer'

Come to me and drink out of me,
and you will not be thirsty, ever.

Bhagwan

It is time to take a more comprehensive look at that elusive subject matter, the experience of being a sannyasin. We look at the backgrounds of sannyasins and at why people have been drawn to Rajneeshism. What are their experiences of actually taking sannyas? We then explore the attractions which keep the sannyasins attached to their chosen path. We also look at why a not inconsiderable number have left the movement.

Drawing on his research of the Medina community, Mullen suggests that

> the average Rajneeshee is 'middle-class', well educated, professionally qualified, has been divorced at least once, has suffered a 'personal crisis', has been through mysticism, drugs, politics, feminism and is 'thirtyish'—in short, the counter-culturalist brought up to date'. [1]

A more detailed picture is provided by a study of the Rajneeshpuram ashram. [2] Slightly over half of those attracted are women. Most of those coming to the ashram were already married. Very few report having been through a divorce. Three quarters of the total population are childless. As for educational attainments, the great majority (over 80 per cent) had been accepted at a university. Over 60 per cent of the ashram have university degrees. Concerning social background, 80 per cent spoke of professional or white collar home environments. Careers before joining the ashram appear to have been relatively satisfactory: only a small number mention unemployment; over 90 per cent think that they had been 'successful' in their work; almost

60 per cent had been earning between 10,000 and 40,000 dollars a year. Finally, most were not brought up in devout religious environments, and in answer to the question, 'Prior to becoming a sannyasin would you have characterized yourself as religious?', 60 per cent answered in the negative.

A third picture is provided by our own study of the twenty or so sannyasins living in Lancaster and High Bentham at the beginning of the 1980s.[3] As at Medina and Rajneeshpuram, they were predominantly 'thirtyish'. Some, mainly ex-students, had been living an alternative lifestyle. This often included activities to do with personal growth. Others, however, had been leading quite conventional lives, firmly attached to their jobs and families. A significant number of the total had working-class backgrounds. Few had been interested in religious or spiritual matters.

There might be such a thing as the 'average' Rajneeshee, but our overall impression is that Bhagwan has attracted a rather mixed bag of people. It should be born in mind that sannyasins are found in many countries, including Japan, India, Australasia, the Americas, Holland, Switzerland, Germany, and even the Soviet Union.[4] Cultural and social factors make it unlikely that the same kind of person is going to be attracted in these different settings. It should also be remembered that sannyasins include the young and the old. Thus the majority of the thirty or so under-sixteen-year-olds at Medina had taken sannyas. Sannyasins also include the penniless and the wealthy, like Prince Welf of Hanover or Sheela Silverman. One sannyasin, Pankaj, told us:

> I come from a working class background. I used to live in London. I have no academic qualifications and after school I did labouring jobs mostly, along with some part-time teaching. I didn't come from a religious background and before I heard about sannyas I had no contact with spiritual groups.

We also spoke with the ex-chaplain of Churchill College, Cambridge, a widely-read man, interested in spiritual and psychotherapeutic matters, and obviously from a very different background.

The diversity of people attracted to Bhagwan means that we cannot provide a simple explanation of his appeal; of why people take sannyas. It is extremely unlikely that such a mixed bag have been attracted for the same reasons. Counterculturalists might well have been attracted by Bhagwan's emphasis on freedom and spontaneity and his embrace of Western psychotherapy. Others, much more firmly attached to the status quo but feeling that there is something missing in their lives, might be attracted by Bhagwan's offer of love. Yet others, relatively happy with their lives, only come to be attracted when a chance encounter with Rajneeshism triggers the realization that this is what they must have. Then there are those who are spiritual seekers, gravitating to Bhagwan the guru; those who are desperate and turning to whatever is at hand; those of a narcissistic bent, attracted by the apparent hedonism of 'life as celebration'. The following personal testimonies show how various people have felt stirred to take the (often) radical step of joining Bhagwan.

Our first testimonies have to do with what has probably been the most significant conversion process, whereby people interested in psychotherapy and the growth movement have come to experience Bhagwan's presence. It is significant because of the large number of people who have been attracted in this fashion. [5] It is also significant because this form of conversion has supplied Rajneeshism with a ready supply of psychologically skilled workers. It will be seen that those attracted through the growth movement are not limited to counter-culturalists nor to those with spiritual aspirations:

> I was working as a Child Care Officer in London in a unit for disturbed kids. After two or three years of this I began to feel that nothing was really happening. A lot of time, care, money, energy and love was being put into these kids, but in fact when they left the unit they still had difficulties. Nothing had fundamentally changed.
>
> So I began to feel that the only way I could ever get greater insight into what we should be doing was by increasing my own insight; by plucking up enough courage to do some encounter groups. I first became involved with Bhagwan by doing groups. It just so happened that one of the group leaders had recently taken sannyas. The idea of a guru or a Master was a very alien concept to me. It didn't fit into any compartment I had ever heard of. It didn't compute. So I listened to the guy talking, and thought 'Well, I'll try to understand what he's saying.' And then sometimes I would find that while my mind was tussling around with what he was saying I would be in tears listening.
>
> But I still couldn't get any connection with Bhagwan. What I did have was a connection with the other sannyasins I met. I found them much more alive, dynamic, powerful and open than any of the other people I was meeting. It wasn't that I particularly liked all their personalities, but they all had an extra spark.
>
> Then one day it just clicked with me that I had to go to Poona. I had to meet Bhagwan and take sannyas. It wasn't a decision for me

because my mind was still objecting. But somehow there was another part of me that could see that my past allegiances were beginning to crumble, anyway. So one day, despite my mind, I gave my notice in and went. I went not really knowing what I was going to do at all. Somewhere the connection had just been formed. Something beyond my reason, beyond my intellect, had just grabbed me. It had plucked me out of what I had been doing. I was incapable of denying it. It was like being in love with someone without being able to say exactly why. I realized that I was in love with Bhagwan in a way that felt very different to anything I had experienced before. During those early days at Poona, I would sit through lectures in the morning, not really knowing why I was there. I just knew that I had to be there. I would see Bhagwan and be in tears: it was like having an overflowing of emotion.

(Sharna)

I moved to England from South Africa with my wife and two children twelve years ago. At that time the Growth Movement was taking off over here and I first heard of Bhagwan through sannyasin group therapists. I found the groups that I did with them were unlike anything I had done before, and realized that I had previously never been honest with myself. I then meditated, read Bhagwan's books and thought he was amazing. Although I kept putting it off, in the end I just jumped into sannyas.

I was given sannyas in England by a sannyasin doctor who used to prescribe Dynamic Meditation as part of therapy.

Later I went to Poona. This involved one of the hardest things I have ever had to do as a sannyasin: reaching the decision to take my fourteen- and sixteen-year-old kids out of school and over to India with my wife and myself. But I had to go.

(Neeraj)

I had been searching for something I couldn't find. I was brought up in the Church of England, and I had for a long time gone to Sunday services. I couldn't make it mean anything, but I couldn't drop it either. So I thought 'Okay, I have to find it for myself, whatever it is. What is life about? What is death about?' I felt that anyone else was really in the way. All the moralizing of the Church services just didn't work.

I first heard of Bhagwan when I started doing groups in London. They were run by sannyasins. But it didn't really mean a lot until I actually went to Poona. That was just part of a travel adventure, but Poona was certainly the first place my husband and I called at. Being in contact with Bhagwan and hearing him speak was a revelation. Everything that I had previously felt about Jesus didn't really help—not in comparison to Bhagwan's interpretations and his living energy. I never made a conscious decision to take sannyas. I went to darshan and that was it. It never felt anything but okay; everything he said seemed as if I had always known it but not consciously.

(Vachana)

I was a chaplain at Churchill College, Cambridge. Before that I was chaplain at Warwick University. I heard about Bhagwan because I was pursuing my own interest in psychotherapy. Long ago, at Warwick, I had arrived at the conclusion that my ministry was missing something. Psychotherapy seemed to offer something to me. In London I came across sannyasins whilst in holistic group situations. One of them suggested I read *The Mustard Seed*, a book on Jesus by Bhagwan. I was terribly moved by it. Then later on I had the chance to go to India. I went to Poona, just to see what this man was like. I was curious; I had no intention of becoming a sannyasin. When I got there I was struck dumb by the man and took sannyas.

(Chinmaya)

Accounts of this variety are legion. Perhaps because of fashion, perhaps because of a sense of adventure, because of some sort of distress, or because they have felt something missing from their work, religion, or life, people have been attracted to the human potential movement. Once on the growth circuit they have chanced upon sannyasins. The experiences which can then result are such as to prompt the people concerned to seek out the source of it all. In the past this seeking has often been legitimated by widespread acceptance in the growth movement that 'Poona is one of the world's largest therapy and growth centres; it must be worth seeing'. Courses put on by sannyasins do not have the same standing today. But some idea of the extent to which they still serve as a conversion route can be gleaned from the fact that on average between thirty and a hundred non-sannyasins every week were attracted to courses put on by Medina in 1984.

Not all who participate in sannyasin groups undergo powerful experiences. It is clear, though, that for some the intensity generated by group work, combined with the interpretations provided by sannyasins, have been an important factor in leading them to Bhagwan. Time and time again, sannyasins say that in groups they came to understand for the first time the real significance of being a sannyasin. Among these sannyasins is Dayananda. His testimony graphically illustrates the role played by group-triggered experiences:

> In the group for the first time I felt the presence of Bhagwan. The way I explain it is the feeling I get overwhelmed with in his presence-godliness. Putting it intellectually, in the group I recognized the link between his existence and my awareness of my own divinity. In the group I was really touched. I felt I had got such a lot from it because of the love within it. Love that was traceable back to Bhagwan. I came away feeling hooked.

Of course, by no means all those attracted to Bhagwan have come by way of the growth movement. Many have simply met sannyasins in the course of their daily lives, or have had friends or loved ones who have taken sannyas. Indeed, Dayananda is a case in point. Only after knowing sannyasins for some considerable time did he decide to participate in a group. For the most part, the appeal here is what is perceived in those who have already surrendered to Bhagwan, particularly in those recently returned from Poona or Rajneeshpuram. Another sannyasin, Vachana, said: 'Their energy was just sparkling from being with Bhagwan. Of course, it wears off, but it was amazing to be with them.' She continued, 'you can feel people are picking up on it.'

It is not as though sannyasins go out of their way to impress others. Rajneeshees emphasize that they do not pressurize people to join them. They see their role as simply being positive and available to the interested. Quite normal personal contact can serve to catalyze change in others. What matters, as far as appeal is concerned, is that they appear to those who come into contact with them as having found an answer; as having a willingness to change and to grow; as somehow being different to the mainstream in a challenging way.

Catalysts have not been limited to sannyasins. Some of those who have been attracted to Bhagwan report their first sense of a connection with him from seeing his picture. (Such people have not always known the identity of the man portrayed when they felt his pull.) Others say they came to know him through his books. Then there are those (not many) who claim that their first experience of Bhagwan took a distinctly unusual form. Dian Raj speaks of having a dream in which he was initiated by a Master. He later recognized that the dream image had been of Bhagwan. In similar vein, another individual, Karen, tells the story of seeing the face of an unknown person whilst practising a Silva Mind Control process. A few months later she happened to have her first encounter with a Rajneesh Meditation

Centre. She was shocked to see a picture of the same man. She flew to Poona to meet Bhagwan in the flesh a short time afterwards.

There are many routes in Bhagwan. The testimonies which we have collected also suggest a high element of chance in whether or not people find their way to him. Relatively few consciously sought out Bhagwan as part of a spiritual search. The majority more or less stumble onto his path:

> I went to India because I was somehow dissatisfied with my life; it wasn't enough anymore. There was always this feeling that there must be something else. I didn't go consciously looking for a guru; I went on an adventure, I guess. Just exploring life. I ended up settling in Bombay. I made a lot of friends and life was pretty good. Bhagwan was unknown to me. However, I started seeing sannyasins. What was striking was that there was something very clean, fresh and attractive about them.
>
> I remember one day stopping a sannyasin in a juice bar and asking what it was all about. I was given Bhagwan's address . . .
>
> (Divya)

> I went to Poona just for a change of scenery. I didn't go to find a Master or anything like that. But I saw Bhagwan and I took sannyas. I only went for a three day holiday!
>
> (Pankaj)

Sannyasins often talk of their conversions as almost accidental. There is an 'out of the blue' flavour to many accounts. They also tend to see their conversions as inevitable. Talk of inevitability probably owes something to Bhagwan's teaching that he has been responsible for setting in motion the train of events which lead people to sannyas. He has said, 'The moment you take sannyas, you think that you are taking sannyas. In the majority of cases I have chosen you—that's why you take sannyas. Otherwise you would not have been able to take such a risk.'[6] It could also owe something to the strong feeling, reported by a great many sannyasins, that they have been impelled to take sannyas:

> I was moving furniture to make room for a political meeting. And this voice came into my head really, really clearly. It said 'You're crazy, you should be in Poona'. I listened to it. I was totally open to sannyas but I didn't know it. I found myself dyeing my clothes red, but to anyone who asked 'What are you doing this for, are you becoming a sannyasin?' I would say 'I don't know' and I would laugh. I went

to Poona. I was doing something totally illogical, totally impulsive.

(Simant)

Simant's 'mind', we might say, found the episode quite unexpected and not worthy of serious consideration; outside her perceived self-image and her notions about what the future entailed. Her 'being' responded differently. It felt drawn to Poona as if by fate.

Hearing voices is unusual. More frequently sannyasins report having been swept away by their emotions. As Pankaj told us, 'The reason I took it came directly from my heart. It was love.' Few can do other than point to an emotional pull to explain why they have taken sannyas. Some can (for example, those self-consciously seeking a spiritual Master or those attracted by the communal philosophy), but most talk of being 'grabbed'. As Pankaj went on to say, 'I cannot think of a rational explanation for it'.

Taking sannyas is rarely guided by rational consideration. Frequently, in fact, the act runs counter to where reason points. Recall Sharna and 'my mind was still objecting'. Or think of Neeraj, who went to Poona despite having to take his children out of school and facing 'sensible advice' from a relative. (Neeraj says 'I had to work out what to do by myself, without relying on social pressures or personal considerations'.) From a different perspective, when people resist the pull of the path of Bhagwan it is often because they are swayed by rational considerations.

Some who have become sannyasins initially fought their impulse to be initiated. Resistance is attributed to dislike of religion; to the feeling that accepting a new name and wearing red clothes and a mala is unnecessary; to the fact that sannyas does not fit in with previous lifestyles; to an unwillingness to surrender to another human being, however impressive. They report feeling afraid of the changes anticipated in becoming sannyasins. An interesting twist to this is that sannaysins often observe that 'he who fights hardest falls furthest'. In other words, many of those now most steadfast in their loyalty to Bhagwan felt they had good reason not to take sannyas and to fight their attraction before 'jumping' into discipleship.

But what of those who do not jump? What of those who remain attached to their 'sensible' way of living? Part of the answer provided by Bhagwan is that he has not chosen them to follow him, perhaps because they are not part of the band of disciples he had nurtured through successive lifetimes, perhaps because they are not ready to make the commitment this time round. Another explanation of why people chose not to take sannyas is found in Bhagwan's exposition on his religion.

> The second category in our religion will be known as 'Shravakas', which means 'listener', and symbolically means 'sympathizer'—although not courageous enough to be a disciple.
>
> The first category is courageous: those who are ready to jump into the unknown and become disciples. The second category is not, but they have the potential to become neo-sannyasins. [7]

Courage is seen as an essential quality in a sannyasin. Those without courage inevitably find that rational considerations outweigh their impulse to jump. Their 'minds' are playing perpetual survival games.

What happens when people decide to take the plunge? Details vary. Until recently, the most common sequence began with the sannyasin-to-be adopting 'orange' clothes. Since colours have come to include pink, red, purple, and mauve, as well as orange itself, initiates will probably consult sannyasin friends to see which colour is currently in favour. (This depends on information provided by a colour chart issued by Rajneeshpuram and subject to seasonal revision.) Typically, on donning the clothes for the first time sannyasins report feelings of self-consciousness, of standing out from the crowd. Nandana comments on a feeling of a new-found sense of freedom in everyday life and describes a commonplace experience, the sensation that 'when you put on orange, things start happening very fast'.

Initiates then approach local Rajneesh centres more formally. Representatives of Bhagwan ask them to meditate for at least a month on a daily basis. Once this requirement is fulfilled, and if the representative feels they are ready for the next step, they are given an application form. The forms, complete with details of name, age, occupation, and so on, and a photograph, are then sent to Rajneeshpuram. In the ensuing weeks, initiates learn if they have been given the go ahead.

The ceremony, as it has been performed at Medina, is a relatively brief affair. It is led by a Rajneeshee minister, is emotionally charged, and possesses little ritual elaboration. One or more initiates join a group of sannyasins to begin the celebration. They sing and dance. Then, one after another, they receive their malas. The malas are felt to encapsulate the very spirit of sannyas. Each mala, as a sannyasin told Bob Mullen, is taken to be 'a gift from [Bhagwan] and a picture of someone we love. Simultaneously it is representative not of a person but of our potential.' [8] Each necklace of one hundred and eight

Experience.

wooden beads, complete with a photograph of Bhagwan, serves as a device to focus the wearer on the present. The mala says: 'the past has gone'. It is a visual manifestation of the inner and immediate relationship that exists between disciple and Master.

Having received their mala, the initiate is given a new name. Male names begin with the prefix 'Swami', meaning 'lord', female with 'Ma', meaning 'mother'. There are two other components to each name. Some see their names as reflecting or mirroring their identity. Others believe the names signify what they have yet to attain. Still others attribute no particular meaning to their name. Like the mala it is just another symbol of their commitment to Bhagwan. Quite a few would agree with Dayal, who told us, 'My first reaction was to wonder how to pronounce my new name'. Before the joyous singing and dancing which marks the close of the ceremony, the initiate receives a personal message from the Master. A typical example, given to Dayal, runs:

Love, be compassionate, share whatsoever you have. Share your very being and don't be a miser. That's the way of sannyas.

Once initiated, the expectations of newly-fledged sannyasins may have to be revised. People often take sannyas with normal ego-dominated expectations of change in mind. As Weechee told us, 'I thought that as a result I would become an improved person with all my positive fantasies intact and all my negativity gone. How wonderful it was going to be! It was nothing of the sort.' Her expectations were dashed because she came to realize that sannyas is not so much about changing the substance of life as it is about changing how life is experienced:

My personality hasn't changed. Perhaps I am lighter. But sannyas has nothing to do with changing the personality and becoming more good. It's about a transformation in the experience of life. Bhagwan actually said to me that it was about relaxing. We live in such an incredible world, but people do such ugly things. Instead of me trying to change them, though, Bhagwan tells me to change the quality of my own life. This then has the consequence of transforming others, but that's not why I do it.

Perhaps the majority of sannyasins, however, find their experiences to be more in tune with their prior expectations. These sannyasins often talk about personal and emotional riches. The quality of their lives has been greatly enhanced. Neeraj sets the tone when he told us,

To me the most fundamental question I could be asked about

Rajneeshism is 'what is the quality of your life?' The answer is that, compared to ten years ago, it is immeasurably rich, and that this richness is still growing.

Dayananda testifies, 'Being a sannyasin has made my life a lot easier. There's more acceptance in me and emotionally I've grown a lot.' Sharna also attaches importance to growth. He told us:

> I know a lot has really changed for me since I took sannyas. Now the pace of life astonishes me. I really love the change around sannyas. It's alive, so you've got to be alive.

His commitment to sannyas has been cemented by this feeling of new horizons. He is particularly disparaging of his past environment:

> Old friends who are not sannyasins still seem to be doing the same things they were doing years ago. There is a feeling of stagnation in them.

Most sannyasins seem to experience 'growth'. For Chinmaya 'growth is what we are all here for'. Dayal tells us, 'The most important thing in life is personal growth in the sense of being happier and more aware.' Sometimes, indeed, it is not so much growth as it is experiencing things for the first time. Divya talks of 'sensitivity' in this fashion:

> Bhagwan helps us to bring sensitivity into our own lives because he has that quality. It's like being given a massage for the first time, realizing that our shoulders are tense and then going deeper and deeper.

It is impossible to do justice to the variegated experiences of sannyasins. Minimally, sannyasins experience change, described by Dayal as 'the scariest and the most exciting thing' about the path. This generally goes together with a sense of personal development, including much of what it is to live as a new man (a topic returned to in the next chapter). There is an increased awareness of potentials in living, not just for the individuals concerned, but also in terms of mankind as a whole. Certainly Sharna experiences the path in terms of what it can teach others. Talking of the creation of more beauty and of a more elevated lifestyle, he describes the Ranch as 'the greatest experiment of all'. 'It shows', he says, 'what man is actually capable of, rather than what he normally does with his resources, which is destruction'.

But what of the experience of purely spiritual progress? It is interesting that few talk of enlightenment as the goal which sustains allegiance. As Weechee formulated it, sannyasins are taught that 'thoughts of enlightenment prevent the experience of what is happening right now'. Perhaps we can say that enlightenment is too remote an experience for the average sannyasin to count as experientially significant. As Bhagwan has continually said, his sannyasins have not arrived at this state of being.

This does not mean, however, that spiritual experiences are insignificant. They are extremely important, hinging as they do on the experience of love. Time and time again we have been told of the heightening of this experience. Simant is representative: 'I feel I am discovering more and more love the longer I am in sannyas. I really don't think that I actually experienced love at all before I became a sannyasin.'

Bhagwan's love is responded to as unconditional and overflowing. It is experiences of the kind reported by Chinmaya and Vachana which lie at the very heart of the path:

> When I was standing back from the crowd on a little rise on a hill, his car passed, he saw me and lifted his hand. I just burst into tears at the loving look. If someone had said this to me a few years ago, I would have said 'You're a silly drip'. But I'm not a drippy sort of person. This man just oozes love, grace, and some sort of energy.
>
> (Chinmaya)

> He is the only person whose presence I've been in who is totally different from anyone else. There is no ego there, no fear, there is nothing. He seems totally available, open to you. I feel incredibly happy, say at satsang, or whenever I see him. It's like a rush of energy. Laughing and crying, all the feelings are there of joy and longing. It's like being in love but it's more.
>
> (Vachana)

Whether physically with Bhagwan or not, this love is there. Divya puts it neatly: 'Every sannyasin carries Bhagwan's love with them. They can at any time tune in and feel nourished, knowing that they have their Master there.'

The experiences we have been discussing are clearly of the variety to bind people to Bhagwan. It seems incontestable that the quality of life is such as to greatly weaken the hold of whatever doubts and criticisms sannyasins might arrive at. Almost all who have been to Poona, Medina and Rajneeshpuram in their heydays have been struck by the great *joie de vivre*. As researchers we can vouch for the sheer exuberance of life at Medina and the Ranch. We can also attest to the fact that sannyasins have continually told us that their experiences more than outweigh the significance of those criticisms (such as financial irregularities and exploitation) which they might have heard. One sannyasin, to give an example, says

> I have a connection with Bhagwan that is beyond what I think or feel about it. Sometimes you hear rumours about him—but they don't touch my connection with him. And when I heard him talking again I thought it was pretty boring actually. But again, that's irrelevant to my connection with him.

Another sannyasin, Sharna, is more explicit in the formulation of what keeps him on the path. For him, proof of its value is provided by the quality of his own life, not by arguments to do with the authenticity of Bhagwan:

> Some people say 'How do you know that Bhagwan is enlightened? Where is your proof?' But there is no proof. Unless you are enlightened, how can you possibly recognize an enlightened person? It's like asking a blind man to describe the difference between red and yellow, or light. All you can do is look inside and say 'has anything happened to me?' It has.

Talking of the 'strength' of the path, Simon Winchester of the *Sunday Times* goes so far as to say,

> while Moonies may resign, and followers of the Maharaj Ji may be deprogrammed and while defections afflict almost all other Masters and gurus, great and small, adherents of the Bhagwan Rajneesh seem unshakable in their beliefs and content in all they do.[9]

The nature of the ties between Bhagwan and his sannyasins certainly appear to support Winchester's observation. As of 1984, an estimated 300,000 have weathered those moments of doubt which must have arisen.[10] Together with the experienced benefits of remaining in the movement, there is a strong feeling that nothing can be gained by leaving. The logic here is that doubt surfaces when the 'spanner in the works' (the ego) feels threatened. To give in to doubt is to give in to the mechanisms of ego-survival—the result being that the ego benefits at the expense of meditativeness and aliveness.

Doubts do not often lead to radical questioning by those committed to Bhagwan. However, the fact remains (and here we diverge from Winchester) that there has been a steady trickle of sannyasins leaving the movement. We take it as axiomatic that sannyasins are not programmed in the sense of being unable to question their allegiance. *All* the sannyasins we have talked with, and this numbers hundreds, have shown critical acumen. Dayananda is representative: 'I guess I feel it's always been important that the things I belong to are "right". If I thought the movement was evil, I would leave.' Indeed, it is this questioning spirit which has resulted in the steady trickle of those dropping sannyas. For example, it is because members at Medina remained questioning that one third of them were not prepared to make the journey to the continent. It is because the new religion, Rajneeshism, has appeared too much like a conventional, organized religion that some 5 per cent of sannyasins in the UK have left the path. It is because of increasing regimentation that approximately half of the twenty sannyasins resident in Lancaster in 1979 have dropped sannyas and become involved in other spiritual activities. It is possible that recent developments have forced many sannyasins to yet again reconsider their commitment.

Whatever the specific reason given—dislike of Sheela, for example, or belief in Sheela's criticisms—the majority who leave explain their departure in terms of 'having lost their connection with Bhagwan'. They no longer feel his presence. This accords with what Bhagwan has to say on the matter: 'once I have withdrawn, sooner or later you will drop sannyas'.[11]

We have ended this chapter with the theme of departure and disaffiliation. Bhagwan's 'magic' or 'presence' is not without limitations. However, it says much of his appeal that very few who go express hostility towards him.[12] Most drift away, retaining some measure of sympathy for the movement and affection for their former guru. They feel sannyas may be wrong for them, perhaps because it has changed too rapidly for their taste. On the other hand, they will say that it is 'right' for those who remain. Some even return to take sannyas for a second time. And in the height of the present troubles, which will undoubtedly generate some exodus, there are still those intent on taking sannyas.

5
Daily Life in the Communal Buddhafield: 'An Experiment to Provoke God'.

The new commune will create a life-affirming religiousness. The motto of the new commune is:
This very body, the Buddha;
this very earth, the Lotus Paradise.

Bhagwan Shree Rajneesh

Communal Buddhafields provide the long-term environment in which Bhagwan works as a 'context-setter'. That is to say, these communities are designed to allow his sannyasins to blossom into maturity. They are the ultimate technique of transformation, providing a continuous setting to provoke surrender. Thus they go much deeper, for example, than communes simply designed as ways of going back to nature.

Buddhafields are seen as having an 'energy' greater than that of any particular member. It is this, says Bhagwan, that accelerates the progress of participants. The 'energyfield' emanating from Bhagwan and functioning as 'the most pregnant force in the world'[1] is somehow heightened when sannyasins live together. Although Bhagwan has never visited the vast majority of his communes, his 'energy' is very much present in all. Characterizing life in the communal Buddhafields, Bhagwan has pronounced:

> There will be consciousness and there will be love, and they will not be contradictory to each other but complementary. Love will give you joy, consciousness will give you crystallization. Consciousness will make you aware of who you are, and love will make you aware of what this world is. And between these two banks the river of life flows.[2]

Until recently, 10 per cent of sannyasins have lived in the communes. (The rest live in sannyasin households or individually.) Revolving around Rajneeshpuram, there are centres as far away as Mauritius, South Africa, New Zealand, and South America. The centres are all highly attuned to one another. In practice this means that they are virtually duplicates of Rajneeshpuram. Whichever commune you visit the catering section will be called Magdelana, the hairdresser is known as Chiyono, and medical attention is dispensed from Pythagoras. Breakfast bowls are arranged in the same fashion, toilets are cleaned according to the same procedure, throughout all specifics. At least until very recently, Rajneeshpuram has provided guidance on organizational details. Rapid dissemination of information ensures that the system remains unified. Organizational attunement, not to speak of frequent messages from Bhagwan (in the form of videos), helps sannyasins to feel that they are living in the unified Buddhafield of their Master. Sense of unity is further enhanced by personal mobility between centres.

Historically speaking, Poona provided the initial impetus for the network. As one sannyasin, Sharna, has told us, 'in Poona energy accumulated until there was enough of it to explode all over the world'. Energy then came to be focused in Rajneeshpuram, the commune we now look at more closely. [3] We look at the project to build 'an oasis in the desert'; at the experiment to create a solution for the crisis facing mankind; at the establishment of a framework to nurture the New Man.

Since its inception in 1981 great strides have been taken to transform over one hundred square miles of virtually empty land (more than twice the area of San Francisco) into a fertile haven. It had previously been a cattle ranch. The soil was eroded, poorly irrigated, and severely overgrazed. The site was deliberately chosen, not because it was cheap, but because of the ecological damage it had suffered. It provided a challenge for the transformative spirit. At the time of purchase only 400 acres were considered suitable for dry land farming of hay and grains and only 300 acres were thought able to support irrigated crops. In order to rectify the situation, the sannyasins followed Bhagwan's instructions:

> The way to regain the balance of nature is not by renouncing technology. It is not by becoming hippies, no, not at all. The way to regain the balance of nature is through superior technology, higher technology. [4]

In this spirit the latest ideas were brought to bear on the site. Where the sannyasins lacked the necessary expertize outsiders were contracted in to help.

By the end of 1983 the Rajneeshees had succeeded in cultivating about 2,700 acres. Wheat, barley, oats, and Austrian peas had been planted. Over 150 acres had been set aside for fodder for dairy cows and beef cattle and 80 acres were under vegetables and green manure crops. There were vineyards, orchards, and a herb garden. Gurdjieff Dam, holding 350 million gallons of water in Krishnamurti lake, was built. Stream beds were repaired to prevent further erosion and several thousand willow trees were planted along the creek beds to assist their recovery. Having thereby ensured a steady water supply and reversed the process of erosion, the Rajneeshees implemented sprinkler irrigation. The water could be put exactly where it was needed, without waste. In this way, the Rajneeshees have laid down the foundations for self-sufficiency, and for an increasing surplus in some crops.

Together with the crops animal husbandry has expanded. The dairy herd, for example, is housed in a technologically advanced barn containing a methane digester producing fertilizer and gas. Technology might be in evidence, but it is not allowed to run amok. The emphasis is on ecological appropriateness. Thus emus, not guns, have been acquired by the sannyasins as the best method of countering attacks on their poultry by scavenging coyotes. And instead of battery techniques, hens are encouraged to lay eggs by providing them with productive listening: Bhagwan tapes, sannyasin, and classical music.

Having laid down the agricultural base for their community, the sannyasins set about building themselves a city complete with every amenity. The design has again taken both technological and ecological considerations fully into account. Constructed on over 2,000 acres of completely infertile land, it is planned that 4000 Rajneeshees will live there by the year 2000. The sewerage system is one example of how technological expertize has been married with the philosophy of respecting environmental resources. Sewage is recycled by being pumped up to two huge pools where it is naturally purified. From there it is used to irrigate the pasture land. Seventy-five per cent of all waste is, in fact, recycled, including food, wood, bottles, and cans. Even oil from the Buddhafield Transport buses is put to use again, heating the garage.

The public transportation system also reflects the concern of the Rajneeshees with the environment. Six miles of new roads have been added to the thirty-five miles of existing road and along them run buses which are both plentiful and convenient. The commune also has its own airline which supplements the bus service to and from Portland, the nearest city.

By the end of 1984 houses had been built for most of the two thousand residents. There is a shopping mall with a bookstore, a hairdresser, a travel agency, clothes and accessories shops, and a shoe shop. Other enterprises include a carpenter, a computer software facility, and a jewellery shop. There is a self-service cafeteria which is free to the residents. There are other outlets catering for a variety of tastes: from Zorba the Buddha gourmet fare to Zorba the Buddha pancakes and ice cream. (These eating places are all vegetarian. Beef cattle that have been introduced are not for home consumption.) Excepting the cafeteria, payment is made with Rajneeshee credit cards.

The Rajneesh International Meditation University has also been built. It offers meditation courses and therapies to visitors to the ranch. Bhagwan has had a house built for him in the secluded Lao Tzu Grove, and a library has been constructed to house his complete works. There is the medical clinic Pythagoras, and an administration building called Socrates which houses the elected city council and the planning and legal offices. Rajneeshpuram has a newspaper, a police force (although it claims to be the only crime-free city in America), firemen, rubbish collectors, a casino, a nightclub, and a mayor. It lacks only two institutions to be found in most cities. There are no nurseries. Women have been asked to give up the distraction of having babies so that they can focus their attention on Bhagwan's vision. Neither are there schools. Those children born before the edict against breeding came into being go to a Rajneeshee school in Antelope. The children have painted the building and selected the furniture: wall-to-wall carpeting, executive chairs and clipboards, tables and sofas.

For a school such interior design is singular, but it is in keeping with the aesthetic and affluent bent found throughout the whole commune. All the interiors in Rajneeshpuram are decorated and arranged so as to convey an immensely relaxing and comfortable environment which only just falls short of the luxurious.

The massive programme of construction and development, which has produced not only a marked improvement in the quality of the land but also a well-heeled city, has taken a staggeringly short period of time. One factor in this achievement is finance, a point underlined by a favourite Rajneeshee car sticker:

Jesus saves
Moses invests
Bhagwan spends.

The 'Mall': Rajneeshpuram, during the annual world celebration.

Over sixty million dollars have so far been spent on developing Rajneeshpuram into a new age, futuristic environment. Some of this capital has come from the extensive investment portfolio controlled by the Rajneesh Investment Corporation. In addition, disciples from all over the world have been asked to donate whatever possible to the venture. Other communes have sent their profits, sannyasins with everyday jobs have in some cases given a percentage of their wages, and so on. At periodic intervals one or another of Bhagwan's Rolls Royces has been raffled off to provide funds, usually for specific projects.

But money is probably not the most important ingredient in the success story of Rajneeshpuram. Most of the credit goes to the commitment of the sannyasins. Their dedication is total. Working on average a twelve-hour day, seven days a week, and despite the fact that they only receive pocket money (eight or so dollars a week) they surely represent one of the most highly motivated workforces in the world.

Why are the sannyasins so highly motivated? Any answer must surely take into account that they are working in a Buddhafield, enlivened with the presence of their Master. They regard all that they do as acts of worship, to be performed with care, willingness, concentration; as opportunities to express their devotion. At the same time, in keeping with Bhagwan's pronouncements on the dangers of seriousness, the sannyasins work in a convivial atmosphere that undoubtedly enhances job satisfaction. Reinforcing their devotion is the way in which all parts of Rajneeshpuram are designated as temples: the businesses, the police station, the administration buildings, the public toilets, the casino. Nowhere is exempt from this appellation. Wherever they are, then, worship is an appropriate response to their environment. Further reinforcement comes from kneeling down together to chant the Gachchhamis before each working shift begins. This reminds them of the continual presence of Bhagwan, of their place in the commune and of their own spiritual potential. Work, the reader will recall, is meditation; an opportunity to move from the periphery to the centre of being.

The lovingness of the commune also has its role to play in the productivity of the Rajneeshees. It functions as an extension of the love felt in the relationship between each disciple and their guru. Individuals are enveloped in a caring and nourishing environment. Being more emotional and receptive than men, women are believed to be primarily responsible for evoking the qualities of the heart. As Bhagwan says:

I want it [the commune] run by the heart, because to me, to be feminine is to become vulnerable, to become receptive. To be feminine is to allow; to be feminine is to wait. To be feminine is not to be tense and in a hurry; to be feminine is to be in love. Yes, the ashram is run by women because I want it run by the heart. [5]

Most of the heads of temples, called co-ordinators, are in fact women. Love is taken to be the organizing power of the community. People, it seems, work out of love, not because they occupy a position in a hierarchical authority structure:

A Rajneesh commune is not founded on authority, period. It is founded on love and that is how it functions. No authority games, no effort to dominate others, or to make things turn out the way 'I' want them. It really is a cooperative. Co-ordinators exist to help the flow of people and ideas. They are not dominant or higher than other commune members, they serve them. In fact, every member of a Rajneesh commune serves every other. [6]

Another fact which has made a significant contribution to the success of the Rajneeshees is the very practical organization of the commune. Each person has to concentrate on simply one daily activity. Each has a specific job allocated to them and the rest of their needs are met by the commune. The Rajneeshees are free to worship secure in the knowledge that meals are being prepared for them, that their living quarters are being cleaned, and that their laundry is being done. This means that they are better able to work long hours. It means that they are surrounded by concrete evidence of love and care. It also means that their ability to be meditative is enhanced. Their concentration is not broken by thoughts of other things they have to do.

Those sannyasins living at Rajneeshpuram have had one more, fundamental, inducement to work. They have had their Master physically present in their midst as an inspiration. They have been able to bathe in his presence as he ventures out for his daily drive. Alan Gustafson of *The Statesman-Journal* records his impressions:

As if drawn by magnets, more than 1,000 people stop work and converge at the heart of this central Oregon commune. They form a line that stretches far along one of its dusty gravel streets. The colours of their clothes—various shades of purple, reds and yellows—contrast with the drabness of the surrounding barren hills.
Some of the people talk. Others hug. A young boy shouts 'Bhagwan is coming.' And sure enough here he comes, cruising towards the

Farming, Rancho Rajneeshpuram.

sea of red in a silver Rolls Royce. Most of the people clasp hands in front of their faces and await in prayerful meditation.

He drives by the people slowly, one hand on the steering wheel, the other raised in a waving salute. The smile seems to send out a high-voltage connection that melts into the hearts of the believers. He is gone in a matter of minutes. Then, in the afterglow shed by the presence of their 'enlightened spiritual master' the sannyasins embrace or linger in silent meditation. Slowly the line crumbles and they return to work smiling and talking happily. [7]

When Bhagwan began to talk again, daily discourses also helped to cement their sense of inspiration.

We turn now to rural Suffolk, to look at what was until recently the headquarters of English Rajneeshism. Basing our description on fieldwork, we are able to give a more detailed account of what it is like to live within the Buddhafield.

Residents at Medina obviously have had to do without Bhagwan's presence. They have had to content themselves with seeing the videos of his discourses. They also all went to Oregon on an annual basis, to join in one or another of the four major Rajneeshee festivals. The community lived in and around a mock-Tudor manor set in thirteen acres of beautifully kept land surrounded by arable countryside. Nowhere else in the Buddhafield served eggs, chips and beans as part of Wednesday lunch, or offered cream teas on Sunday afternoons. But aside from these snippets of cultural identity, contacts with other centres were close, and particularly contact with Rajneeshpuram.

At the time Medina was established, in September 1981, there were many sannyasins living in England, often in small centres but none in any Poona-style communities. When sannyasins returned to Britain from Poona after Rajneesh moved to America, they felt that they wanted to continue living in a large commune. Bhagwan had also said that they should be his emissaries:

You will be my ambassadors at large, you will function for me. I will see through your eyes, and I will speak through your tongues, and I will touch people through your hands, and I will love through your love. [8]

Accordingly a group of sannyasins, headed by a woman called Ma Anand Poonam, bought Medina. An open invitation was extended to all sannyasins to join them. A number sold what they had and moved in as well. The buildings were purchased for £290,000, the money being raised from donations from newcomers, unsecured loans and a debenture scheme on the property which realized £190,000. Residents with no personal income were paid £5.50 pocket money a week. Otherwise all their needs were met by the commune.

The numbers of those who lived at Medina fluctuated considerably. Until right at the end, though, when there was a last influx of sannyasins from smaller centres which were being closed down, there were generally around 120 adults and 30 children. Some were there as part of the original group. Some had been asked especially to live there because they had skills which were needed by the commune. Some moved there because they felt that they could achieve more, and have a greater sense of their Master, in a group environment. Others just found themselves there and stayed, like one who intended to visit for only two days as a musician and ended up practising law there full time.

The largest building at Medina acted as a focal point for the whole community. Upstairs were sleeping quarters, downstairs was a large kitchen, the cleaning temple, and a cuproom which dealt with an apparently endless flow of crockery to be washed. There was a dining and reception area, offices, and a bar operating under a club licence. Stepping outside the rear entrance revealed a laundry and a shop selling clothes, jewellery, Rajneeshee newspapers, and a range of cigarettes and confectionery. Offices and dormitories adjoined. To the right, through an avenue of carefully tended cherry trees and rosebushes, there was guest accommodation, the 'Kid's House' and some of the businesses set up by the sannyasins. At the bottom of the path lay the Healing Centre where both conventional medicine and alternative therapy was on offer.

In short, Medina had extensive facilities. To support itself it had to live up to its name, which means both 'Holy City' and 'marketplace'. This it did, demonstrating considerable commercial acumen enlivened with a simultaneous sense of worship. All its businesses were profitable, from the British edition of the *Rajneesh Times* newspaper to the graphic design studio and computer software company. Some sannyasins also left the premises to worship. Off site was a print shop and Medina had a travelling construction team. In London a rota of Rajneeshees also worshipped at the Medina-owned 'Body Centre'. From being a Hampstead squash club it developed into a centre for therapy and dance, with a vegetarian restaurant attached.

The temples had comfortable interiors and left visitors in no doubt of the allegiance of those inside. Pictures of Bhagwan were displayed everywhere and either tapes of his discourses or sannyasin music would often be playing. As in Rajneeshpuram, each sannyasin would only do one job each day, the rest of their needs being met by the commune. All the members exuded friendliness and caring for one another. So the Rajneeshee salesmen, whose job involved travelling to get orders for the design studio, would be greeted on their return with hugs from everyone in their temple. In the laundry clothes were folded meticulously so that the wearer could put them on without fuss and feel looked after, and everyone who collected or deposited their wash received caring attentiveness.

Worshippers in the kitchen were reminded before the Gachchhamis were chanted that they should prepare the food for the community with love and that they should feel Bhagwan's presence in their work. They were also enjoined not to lift pots that were too heavy and to be careful when using sharp knives, admonitions which intensified the atmosphere of concern for their well-being. In the same vein, handcream was available in each domestic temple to ensure that the sannyasins felt properly cared for. The Gachchhamis themselves affirmed the sense of camaraderie. As Vachana told us, when the practice was introduced,

> it felt strange and a bit jokey. Could we really do it at six o'clock in the morning when we started our worship, maybe not feeling very good-tempered? Kneeling down and feeling Bhagwan, feeling our togetherness and doing this chanting? But it brought us together. It's quite subtle. It's like a telepathic thing. It softened the energy, I could feel it.

Those who worked away from Medina did not feel isolated despite their circumstances. Hot meals would be cooked daily for the worshippers in the print shop twelve miles away and if possible its members would worship in Medina itself on Sundays, to make them feel part of the community. The construction team, likewise, would return each weekend to the commune to be revitalized, and whilst they were away during the week it was the job of other members of the team to look after them and to make sure that they still felt in touch with 'sannyas energy'.

Whether the sannyasins worshipped at Medina or not, however, they saw their worship as having a variety of benefits. One was the vitality which they felt at work, despite, or perhaps because of, the long hours worshipping. As Divya says,

> When I put my total energy into my worship, that is the time I feel

most fulfilled. I've experimented with that. There is nobody standing around with a big stick. But the more energy you put in, the more satisfied you feel. It's a long time since I had job outside the Commune so it's hard to say, but from what I remember people do nine until five and go home feeling very frazzled. Yet that is actually a very short day compared to what we do here. Somehow we are finding that more energy is there. So to be here for twelve hours a day doing something doesn't seem like a hardship at all. It is a worship. It's becoming sacred. I feel that. And if I am given time off work, if I do get tired, that's fine. But apart from that it doesn't seem that I have the need to take time off.

Another perceived benefit was the growth which many sannyasins felt came out of their worship. Most, unless they had a special skill which takes years to acquire, moved frequently from job to job. One day they might be cleaning cars in the transport temple, the next they could well be worshipping in Accounts. Poonam, who ran Medina until mid-1984, maintained that she simply asked people to do what was required. Nevertheless, job changes gave sannyasins the feeling that they could thereby learn something about themselves. Chinmaya observes,

When I first came to Medina I was a painter. Then I worked with the dustcart, collecting all the rubbish. I did that for about three months. Then I was in the garden, then in the cuproom washing cups. I see that just when I have begun to settle down I have been aroused out of my security again. I was becoming a fairly competent gardener. I knew today what I was going to do tomorrow. But then that was taken away, and to begin with I was angry. I thought 'Why is it that when I am getting on so well in the garden I am moved, and someone who knows nothing of gardening will do the job instead?' In the cuproom I was confined within four walls, washing dishes. I felt it was an awful waste of time. But I could also see that this is what I needed to happen. I needed to be with people after having been isolated in the garden. Coming into the cuproom brought me right into the heart of the community. Now I have just moved into Accounts, and that has been traumatic. Because there is one thing I cannot do, I cannot count figures! I reckon that if I was going to be an accountant in a bank or an office, maybe after a month I might be entrusted to look after certain columns. Here, after one day, I was given twelve columns to look after and the person who preceded me just buzzed off! I can see growth in this.

Such successive changes, and the resistance they provoked, provided, in the eyes of the Rajneeshees, day-long opportunities to surrender. They were seen as a device to help sannyasins lose their conditioned identification with a particular role or identity. In the words of Sharna,

> You don't *become* a boss or an underling, a doctor or an accountant or a cleaner. These are all just jobs you are doing now, and tomorrow you could be doing something completely different. Obviously, there are some people with specific skills which take a long time to acquire. But even they know that they cannot hide behind that role. They do other jobs as well so that all their self images go.

Because the Rajneeshees were all working together towards the same end, the unfolding vision of their Master, they felt it inappropriate to take personal credit for what they had done. Worshipping together, they said, and pooling their resources, produced a result greater than they could have expected to achieve alone. In such ways, they believed, their egos were prevented from feeding on what they had accomplished. Weechee comments:

> I feel that a group of people have an immense energy, more than a single person. Worship has no personal gain. It doesn't gratify the ego. Because I do it in the Commune and the Commune contributes to my worship the end product isn't something I look at and claim as mine. I am a part, but I am not indispensable in the Commune. If I left someone else could and would do my job. Status and personal gain have nothing to do with it. I don't personally get charged up about being an incredibly good writer. All these things are peripheral to the experience.

What appeared central to the experience of the sannyasins at Medina, and indeed is still so at Rajneesh Centres today, was the meditative quality achieved through worship. More and more the sannyasins felt they were able to perform whatever job they had been given whilst remaining undistracted by its apparent 'form', whether, 'nice', 'boring', 'complex', or 'unpleasant', or by their transient emotions.

> When I worship it doesn't matter whatever else is happening in my life. I become absorbed and the ups and downs are irrelevant.
>
> (Weechee)

> The quality of my life with Bhagwan is immeasurably rich. Because in my work life I can be meditative very much easier than I ever have before. And I am aware of other layers of consciousness which I see from time to time.
>
> (Chinmaya)

Everything that Bhagwan said when he was speaking about worship was just 'Go in'. So from the outside you see a bunch of people doing jobs just like in any other commune. What you can't possibly see, except in the fact that these people are incredibly beautiful (and I have seen their transformation from Poona days until now), is this inner quality.

(Simant)

Given that the Rajneeshees at Medina were often put into jobs which they initially had little or no idea how to perform, it might come as a surprise that the commercial side of Medina made any money at all. Yet it did. Medina businesses were making in the region of a quarter of a million pounds a year net profit in 1982. The commune could well afford to support all its members and to send them to Oregon for two weeks of every year, including the children.

Like their parents, most of the children at Medina were sannyasins. The Rajneeshees lived collectively, not separated up into individual family units. This is not to say that the children were not allowed to see their parents whenever they wanted to. The children slept in dormitories in the 'Kid's House' and it was there that the primary school was run. School was in the morning and organized by qualified Rajneeshee teachers. In the afternoon the children joined the rest of the community by worshipping in any one of the temples. This, it was said, gave them a variety of work experiences and made them feel a part of the commune. Some of the children had been sannyasins ever since they could remember. Others had only recently decided to take sannyas. The few who were not sannyasins, however, were not ostracized. Neither was there any overt pressure on the children to believe in Bhagwan and his teaching. Having Bhagwan in their lives was as natural to the children as having their teddies, their parents, and their nightly bedtime rituals of storytelling and massage before the lights were put out. He was simply there.

Although they were not taught about him at school, the children's education was undeniably structured in accordance with his principles. The conventional Rajneeshee attitude to education is that each child should be taught according to their psychological maturity, not on the basis of age. Education should address the needs of the whole individual. Subjects like history and political science are seen as useless and are omitted from the curriculum. Together with basic skills, emphasis was on creative work (painting, poetry and so on). Co-operation not competition was the order of the day. Their academic work was never graded and they never sat any examinations: such assessment was seen to be an undesirable component of standard education, leading to feelings of fear and separation in later life. In matters of discipline the teachers relied on their communicative skills and insight. In the words of one teacher, Satyam: 'None of the children here are punished, and we do not use any kind of violence with them. We talk about whatever is happening and try to clear it up. It may turn out that somehow I've been unfair and then I apologize.'

Apart from the obvious fact that their lives took place in the setting of a Rajneeshee commune and so to an extent were different from those of 'normal' children, Medina kids seemed much like any others. They raced around on BMX bikes, told jokes to anyone who would listen, played football, climbed trees, and scrapped. When the girls were old enough they fell head over heels in love with Boy George. Generally, however, the qualities extolled by their elders were those held dear by the community as a whole: honesty, sensitivity, responsibility for their own emotions in dealing with others, and self-reliance.

What of the adults? Like the children, many of them had by this time known each other for years and genuinely felt as if they were part of the same family. Only a few admitted to loneliness. (In line with Rajneeshee philosophy such people would point out that they knew this was due to themselves and not to the unfriendliness of others.) Most would have concurred with the following description of Medina life made by Chinmaya, who had been there from the start:

> Some people I relate to better than others because they come from similar backgrounds or have similar interests. Some people from time to time irritate me. But at other times they don't irritate me and I see that my earlier feelings were coming from myself. I think that this is what we are all learning, that we project outwards. It would be untrue to say that this is a kind of paradise where everybody loves everybody else. But I've never seen any violence here. Not even people shouting at each other. I think the people here are more emotionally mature. They realize they feel angry but they don't direct it at other people, although we are not afraid to call a spade a spade.

Regarding their intimate relationships, some of the Rajneeshees moved from partner to partner fairly frequently; some settled with just one, sharing a living 'space' with them and the same shelf space in the laundry, and some were actually married. This last state, however, was the exception rather than the norm because, the sannyasins said, their relationships existed only while love existed in them. In contrast to those in the everyday world, their relationships ended when they had naturally ceased to work, instead of continuing through habit or insecurity. Though not true of all relationships at Medina, it was obviously the case for many. Despite this fluidity, relationships were relatively stable. We saw nothing of the sexually rampant behaviour reported of Poona days. This is not to say, however, that sannyasins had become inhibited about expressing their sexual feelings or that they fought shy of the topic. Divya told us, 'our sexual energy' isn't suppressed. Not that we are rampaging about either. But here as well as love for friends there is a sexual love that helps our lives become whole. There is a freedom here, and yet it's not promiscuity.' Sannyasins generally appear more tactile than other sections of the populace, often embracing intensely on meeting, or hugging each other to convey joy or to comfort. The reader will recall, however, that in the aftermath of the revelations concerning AIDS there has been a change in sexual mores.

The first British sannyasin wedding occured in 1984. This was held on St Valentine's Day, in the crowded reception area at Medina. Poonam, as the presiding minister, stood with the intended couple at one end of the room, surrounded by journalists and television cameras. Those assembled sang a sannyasin song, 'Let the sunshine in', and then Poonam explained the significance of the Gachchhamis, amid uproar and laughter when she incorrectly translated the Sanskrit phrases into their English counterparts. Gachchhamis were chanted, jokes were told, Bhagwan's thoughts on marriage were read out, and the couple exchanged rings and wreaths to complete the ceremony; festive dancing, singing, eating, and drinking followed. All in all, both in atmosphere and content, the wedding perfectly exemplified a traditional Rajneeshee celebration. And if weddings have been thin on the ground, there have been other celebrations of one kind or another almost every week at Medina. Birthdays, religious festivals, Guy Fawkes Day, St Valentine's day, New Year's Day, and so on.

At such times numbers swelled. So did they at weekends when visitors would descend on the place: to do groups, see friends, undergo treatment at the Healing Centre, or simply relax and watch a video. During the rest of the time there would also be a handful of visitors on 'Healing Weeks' to revitalize themselves.

Given the number of people at Medina, and the crowding that occurred, life was surprisingly harmonious. The sannyasins slept in dormitories with little privacy. Because of the pressure of numbers, and the fact that they might at any time have to move to London (or perhaps go out with the construction team) each was assigned only a temporary living 'space' for themselves and their few personal possessions. In addition to the residents there were also Rajneeshees attending one-year Rajneesh Therapy courses or courses in practical skills run by the design studio and the garage.

How was all this harmony achieved? Medina, of course, was aesthetically very pleasing to live in. The sannyasins were all there by choice. Furthermore, as Sharna remarked, the very fact that there was little privacy served to enhance their togetherness: 'In worship and at other times you are constantly rubbing up against other people, and all your sharp edges and rigidity have to go. Other people around you are not going to stand for it.' The ethos of loving and nourishment which was so much in evidence at Medina also contributed to the prevention of any breakdown in the prevailing sense of concord. It was constantly visible: in the messages around the commune which began 'Beloved' and ended with 'Love', the standard Rajneeshee format; in the loving reminders that everywhere was a temple for their Master; and in the invocation before the evening Gachchhamis which asked sannyasins to drop any negativity they had felt during the day. Furthermore, instead of being a source of turbulence, visitors would generally quickly get in step with the lifestyle of the place. Indeed, by stepping into such an environment a number were persuaded to take sannyas themselves. Overall there were few sources of threat to the atmosphere of gregariousness and warmth.

Our account so far might give the impression that there were few rules at Medina. This was not the case. There were rules concerning quite small matters, for example forbidding hitch-hiking to and from the commune. An illustration of rules regarding more serious matters is provided by the fact that drug users were warned that if they were caught with drugs on the premises they would be turned over to the local police. Other rules were there to protect the commune. Thus a bead system was introduced to prevent the transmission of sexual disease. Any commune member having sexual relations with outsiders had to wear a green bead on their mala to indicate they were in quarantine for a set period. Non-commune members, after quarantine, were issued with purple beads which declared them free from infection (AIDS prohibitions provide another example of protective rules).

There were also rules which ensured that Medina operated as much like Rajneeshpuram as possible. Orders from the Ranch covered the general to the particular, from the correct method to clean a floor to the outlawing of kissing. The leadership, headed by Poonam, was an additional source of regulation. The gap between their circle and the rest was readily discernible. Under her regime Medina was subjected, in Mullan's words, to 'benevolent dictatorship'.[9] She made policy decisions, unless, that is, Rajneeshpuram took the lead. She ate separately, never joined the community for the evening Gachchhamis, and her office, the inner sanctum, could not be casually entered except by the chosen few. Her instructions were obeyed to the letter and her power was acknowledged by all. Sheela, too, was subject to special attention when in England. A team of sannyasin painters and decorators worked round the clock in the spring of 1984 to prepare quarters for her to an appropriately luxurious standard.

On that visit, Sheela commented that any sannyasin should feel able to approach and talk to her. She asked them not to consider her different from themselves. When Patipada, Poonam's replacement, arrived from Oregon in mid-1984 she reportedly took a screwdriver to the door of the inner sanctum and said that there should no longer be hierarchy in Rajneeshism. But, as Mullan writes, whilst Poonam held sway everyone seemed to like it that way. Few would have changed places with her, and most felt, as Mullan also observes, 'Poonam is the nearest thing to Bhagwan they've got.'[10] Poonam's authority and the regulations she implemented were seen as a necessary part of life. Chinmaya summed it up:

> There are rules here, like the one most people follow of driving on the right hand side of the road. They are those sorts of rules. If we all had motor cars and just drove anywhere I would PRAY for somebody to make a rule so we could all drive safely. That is to say, rules don't restrict my freedom.

Ultimately, those rules which triggered resistance in commune members were also seen as perfect opportunities for surrender.

If sufficiently antagonized by the lack of privacy or the rules a sannyasin could always decide to opt out of Medina. The few who did so, however, usually moved on the grounds that 'I still feel I have things to do in the outside world': money to make, relationships to form, places to go, and the sensation of independence to relish. In the later days of Medina such decisions were accepted uncritically. In earlier times those who had decided to leave apparently felt a hint of judgement in the attitudes of others—and more than just a trace of the belief that somehow those inside the commune were better than those outside, and closer to Bhagwan. The later attitude was that there was no one way of being a sannyasin that was right in itself and that, taking a liberal stance, each must decide which course to take.

The qualities of life at Medina are highlighted by what sannyasins have told us of their attitudes to life in the everyday world. Sannyasins rarely deny that they are able to live in normal society. As Divya told us, 'I could do it, and I would still feel connected to Bhagwan.' She continued, 'it doesn't matter where you are'. But like others she showed little desire to leave the commune. Most paint a disheartening picture of what outside life would be like. Sharna observes, 'Outside, everyone lives in their own little castles. Whatever ego-trips they have, no one is going to call them up.' He continued, in a way which shows how he had come to appreciate what Medina had to offer, 'I used to really treasure privacy. Now that's gone. I don't want a walled-in space of my own.' Divya reports in similar fashion:

> In the commune I have been given experience and training in so much. It would be interesting to go outside and use it. But going back into the family unit seems very barren. There would be love there, but probably just from one person. That feels very narrow.

An account of daily life in the communes would not be complete without mention of how it has been affected by external opinion. The 'experiment to provoke God' has generated a wide range of responses. A number have been favourable. Cheryl Isaacson, enthusing in *Here's Health* magazine, writes:

> I felt when I visited Medina, and still feel, that Rajneesh has a lot to offer, and that the results of following his philosophy—clear-minded, open, full, active, productive people, in most cases—speak for themselves. [11]

Another visitor, a parent, is equally enthusiastic:

> The commune does not represent some evil, mysterious sect. Medina welcomes visitors, especially on Sundays. I'm sure you will come home as I did, relaxed and refreshed by the unusual warmth and openness of the atmosphere of the place. [12]

In response to those who argue that Medina carefully 'stage manages' visits to create a favourable impression Simon Freeman of the *Sunday Times* went behind the scenes. His report lays to rest some of most common accusations levelled at the community. On the night of his visit, and after 'reassured parents had departed', he 'toured the grounds, hoping to find traces of the mass orgies and mass hysteria revealed by other newspapers. In the bar, Rajneeshis sat drinking and smoking (alcohol and cigarettes). A few couples strolled in the pleasant night air.' However, Freeman himself, along with a number of other visitors, has helped to generate an adverse climate of opinion. This in turn has generated disruption in the daily life of the commune. Freeman's criticisms run as follows:

> The manor is strangely unsettling. The Rajneeshis giggle in unison. They are totally unable to countenance criticism of Bhagwan. They are not really interested in anything outside their own community and its business ventures. They have unquestioning group loyalty. For example, after one innocuous conversation with me, the manor's doctor, a seasoned GP, scurried off to report to Ma Poonam. [13]

Andrew McEwan, of the *Daily Mail*, operating undercover, is more savage. He found strange and disruptive elements at work in the heart of the English countryside:

> The house at Herringswell in Suffolk is mock Tudor and couldn't be more beautifully English. But that's the outside. The inside could not be more frighteningly alien. To enter Medina is to risk emerging with values turned upside down, old loyalties broken and a nicotine-like craving to be with the 'guru' or his 'sannyasins'. [14]

Such views have undoubtedly helped turn a number of local residents against the community. Although some neighbours have found the sannyasins friendly, or have adopted a 'live and let live' stance, the majority have been alarmed. Some have been openly hostile. During a meeting of the Forest Heath Planning Committee in April 1984 the community was described as 'a nest of vipers', 'a cancer', and as 'anti-Christ'. [15] The meeting turned down an application for a lecture room extension and for visitors accommodation. (Poonam's response was ironically to refer to the fact that this 'bureaucratic lynching took place during the Easter season, the time when all Christians remember the suffering and death of their Master'.) [16]

Hard on the heels of the planning furore, Medina announced its intention to field candidates for a forthcoming local election. The aim was to ensure fair play in Herringswell. Poonam declared:

> We will represent everyone equally and fairly. We could not trust the local community to do this. Many are windbags and bigots. We are as much a part of the local community as anyone else. The local people

have shown themselves unfit to run the council by their prejudice and repression. [17]

Her opponents feared that the Rajneeshees were attempting a takeover of local politics in order to get their own way.

It is apparent that daily life in Medina could not remain immune from adverse outside responses. The supposedly peace-loving Buddhafield got embroiled in heated and aggressive controversies. It is only fair to say, however, that most commune members felt little pressure to change their normal lives. They might sometimes have been told by Poonam to put on a show when visitors arrived (such as not hugging with normal fervour), but most were not directly concerned with public relations.

In contrast, life at Rajneeshpuram has been radically disturbed by the efforts of outsiders to destroy the community. Opposition derives from two main sources. One is in line with the well-known fact that lifestyles perceived as alien often generate frightening rumours. The level of hysteria surrounding Rajneeshpuram is illustrated by the following: 'I heard that the reason there were no kids on the Ranch was because they were used as human sacrifices. I also heard that they were building missile sites out there.' [18] The second source of antagonism derives from the sannyasins' efforts to extend their sphere of influence beyond the Ranch. Antelope, the nearest town, has had a Rajneeshee mayor and council (meetings of which begin and end with jokes). Two thirds of the original inhabitants have left—perhaps not surprisingly given how their sensibilities have been affected by the appearance of nudity in a local park, not to mention how their prosperity has been affected by a doubling of property taxes. Says one resident, 'They've got a concerted campaign to run roughshod over us, and ramrod through whatever they want to around here. They've got a platoon of lawyers who jump everytime something comes up. They're going for power.' [19]

That the Ranch has contributed to the ailing local economy (one businessman claiming that 1.25 million dollars a month has been spent) has been ignored. Opposition is rife, from car stickers reading 'Better dead than red' to sustained attempts to render the Ranch illegal. Ever since Rajneeshpuram was given city status in the spring of 1982 by Wasco County Court, its standing has been under attack. The 'Thousand Friends of Oregon' group has filed a suit on the grounds that the city is built on agricultural land. The Attorney General of Oregon has favoured the strategy of claiming the Ranch violates the American constitutional separation of Church and State.

Public figures in general have been motivated by the feeling that 'it's not a kiss of death for a politician to be perceived as pro-Rajneeshee, it's a knife through the ribs'. [20] Opposition has also taken the form of actual violence. For example, two bombs were planted in the Rajneesh Hotel in Portland.

Most recently, the viability of the commune has been even more threatened. Its heart has been ripped out by Bhagwan's departure from America. A four-year investigation by Immigration officials has had an effect. Life at the Ranch has increasingly taken on a beleaguered, embattled air. Rajneeshees have had to run an increasingly tight ship. An ex-sannyasin, Susan Harfourche, claims that Rajneeshees of Sheela's time had been trained to repel visits from the FBI. She writes that a complex security system was in operation, to ensure that unwanted visitors were either turned away or prevented from doing any damage. [21] Guards were placed on the perimeters; Bhagwan himself was under twenty-four hour protection from armed sannyasins. The community was under siege. Sheela might have said 'the work continues unaffected by the turmoil, with celebration, with love, with life'. She might have used the image of 'living at the still centre of a cyclone'. [22] One wonders.

What does seem apparent, though, is that the commune has not been destroyed. Stiffened by their ordeals, sannyasins are now talking of strengthening their home. As the President of the Rajneesh Investment Corporation has said: 'We are into pure business now. We are focussing our energies on things that will help the commune.' [23] Mining, previously regarded as 'a non-meditative activity', is now to go ahead.

It is almost as if sannyasins have been drawn into the aggressive down-to-earth life of America; as if opposition has lead them to respond in kind and has forced sannyasins at the Ranch to partly create their own 'garbage'. Is it really the right way to live harmoniously in the world by being continuously provocative? Certainly Sheela succeeded in arousing antagonism wherever she went. We might ask why she was so fond of telling well-publicized jokes along the lines,

How do you fit several hundred Jews into a Volkswagen?

Put two Germans in the front and the Jews in the ashtray.

Small wonder that Beth Hersh of the Jewish Federal Council of Los Angeles responded to this televized joke by saying 'we want them out of the country'. [24]

Since writing this chapter, in December 1985, we have learnt that Rajneeshpuram is in fact being wound down. Rumours abound as to where the sannyasins will go. If talk of a Fijian island, sites in South America or a new ashram in India is true, Hersh's desire might be fulfilled more rapidly than she anticipated.

6

The Rule of Freedom or the Freedom to Rule: 'A Master of Contradiction'

*Fixedness is the nature of the mind
and fluidity is the nature of life.*

Bhagwan Shree Rajneesh

At the heart of Bhagwan's path lies a contradiction. His teachings continually point to a realm beyond mind, beyond ego, beyond concepts, beyond relationships, beyond the social. His teachings point to an experience of absolute freedom. On this Bhagwan is uncompromising:

> Life is freedom. God is absolutely a freedom. You cannot have any fixed attitudes, fixed ideas. If you have them you will be in trouble. [1]

The freedom of Buddhahood, he insists time and time again, is all that matters. Yet his vision has involved all the trappings of a large scale organization. It has involved the accumulation of rules, regulations, commands, rituals, and, it seems, a growing loss of liberty. Despite his repeated admonitions that 'form' stands in the way of the 'formless', Bhagwan appears to have developed more and more form-bound constraints.

This contradiction has been present from the beginning of the movement. In effect, Bhagwan has always said, 'I teach freedom. You take sannyas.' He has always said, 'Surrender your egos and be free, but surrender to me.' He has always said, 'be spontaneous', yet he tells people what to do. As time has gone on the contradiction has gradually become more pronounced. With the appearance in 1981 of Rajneeshism and with the increasingly tight organization of Rajneeshpuram it has almost seemed that the contradiction has been resolved, form winning over the formless, obedience winning over freedom. However, given that Bhagwan has never refuted his earlier teachings on naturalness and spontaneity, and given that his last public words, spoken in 1981 before going into silence, ended with 'You are freedom',[2] we assume that the contradiction has not disappeared. Indeed, we know that it has not disappeared. Since September 1985 Bhagwan was saying that form had come to dominate too much and that much greater emphasis should be given to the realm of the free spirit.

The tension between freedom and obedience has always resulted in problems for sannyasins. Having been attracted to sannyas as a way of gaining liberation from the socialized ego, sannyasins during the 1970s found that they had to accept rules. As we have seen, the ashram at Poona was awash with regulations. Many regarded these as a small price to pay for their new-found sense of expression and aliveness. Others, however, tended to rebel. That sannyasins found it difficult to combine the two aspects of Bhagwan's path is clearly shown by our 1979 study of disciples in Lancaster. 'Disparates' opted for the easy going, spontaneous aspect, treating Bhagwan as a close friend, not setting themselves apart from non-sannyasins, refusing to take anything seriously, not thinking in terms of rules, let alone goals, and in general enjoying whatever came along, whether it be meat, alcohol, cigarettes, the cinema, or the occasional meditation. 'Incumbents', on the other hand, surrendered to Bhagwan rather than to the moment. Their lives were ordered, not unpredictable. They saw themselves following a relatively strictly laid down path towards enlightenment.

As we predicted at the time, Incumbents (or rather a more extreme version of this position) won the day. Disparates became an endangered species. By 1981 newly initiated sannyasins had taken the theme of obedience and discipline yet further. Bhagwan's teachings as an ultimate authority were regarded with devout reverence. Bhagwan's commands were accepted to the smallest detail. Members saw themselves as being radically different from non-sannyasins. The emphasis on rules and obedience was such that even the Incumbents felt estranged and were prompted to become more 'Disparate-like' by emphasizing 'their own thing' and individual responsibility.

We can only suppose that many 'Disparate'—inclined sannyasins the world over became increasingly dissatisfied with developments during the 1980s. The man who had claimed, 'there is no possibility of any society which will be really free'[3] seemed intent on building up an intricate social system in his Buddhafield. The man who had

Hierarchy?

attacked traditional religions on the grounds that organized truth is a lie seemed intent on implementing the new religion of Rajneeshism. The 'guru of free love' introduced rules even into this domain. It must have seemed that what had been 'surrender to freedom' was becoming 'surrender to system', that detachment from form was being replaced by attachment to the dictates of those running the communes.

With the 'the system' winning over freedom, and constraints over spontaneity, the ego came back into its own. As a consequence, many of the evils which Bhagwan has always taught are generated by the ego have come to pass. This is not the authors' judgement. Bhagwan himself now says that his path had fallen prey to form-dominated organization. As he says, Rajneeshpuram under Sheela become 'a concentration camp'. [4] In accord with Bhagwan's teachings on the ego, people at Rajneeshpuram became attached to power. Hierarchical tendencies became pronounced. Barriers appeared. People identified with their positions, which become their prisons. The assertion of power, aggressive attitudes to the outside world, attachment to wealth, paranoiac attitudes and responses (including the acquisition of guns) are all now seen by Bhagwan as the consequence of egos reasserting themselves. Sheela and her associates would no doubt think differently. But the fact remains that the last months of her command showed every signs of system having come to rule. Little was left of the rule of freedom.

Bearing in mind Bhagwan's recent rejection of organization, are we to conclude that the tension between freedom and obedience, formlessness and form, is bound to lead to one side or the other winning out? Is Bhagwan's path inherently unstable, bound to oscillate between the two poles as organization develops and then is rejected?

According to Bhagwan's teachings, roles and obedience are necessary to gain freedom. It follows that if rules and obedience are working well, freedom is increased and the possibility of ego-inspired attachment and 'garbage' consequently decreased. Bhagwan's assertion that,

> I have no pattern to give you,
> no values, no morality,
> I have only freedom to give you
> so that you can flower. [5]

is in many ways compatible with following his commands. Sannyasins find freedom through obedience. Commands and rules, it will be recalled, are held to effect liberation from what is otherwise constraining. For example, sannyasins in communes are often abruptly told to change their job. Possibly having become attached to one job, resisting change, this allows sannyasins to see their egos at work. Or again, Dynamic Meditation only works if you obey the rules of the process. Indeed, all the techniques of transformation, all the ways in which Bhagwan works as a context-setter, depend on obedience to the setting which has been provided. In this sense, then, the contradiction with which we began this chapter is resolved. As a technique, formal injunctions are held to free people rather than attach them to the commands.

But the nature of the relationship between rules and freedom makes it all too easy for system to prevail. What was introduced to facilitate detachment from the ego, not to mention providing freedom from, for example, AIDS or chaotic communal life (someone must have the responsibility for washing the dishes), can only too readily become confining. It is only human nature for people with good jobs to want to keep them. It is only human for those with power not to want to relinquish it.

We postpone discussion of why Bhagwan allowed ego to win until the concluding chapter of this book. For the present we wish to explore the question of why so many sannyasins allowed themselves to become 'prisoners'; why so many well-educated, intelligent sannyasins appear to have been happy to have relinquished much of the freedom which first attracted them to the movement. Putting it more forcefully, we explore why they have not seen that the freedom so often mooted in Bhagwan's teachings is largely absent in recent communal life.

One solution is that enough freedom has been retained to satisfy those with 'Disparate' sentiments. Sannyasins that we spoke to during Poonam's relatively authoritarian regime at Medina tended to emphasize that they had chosen to obey her rule. They talked about their freedom to be 'in the now', about the fact that although hierarchy existed, its force was mitigated by virtue of people being moved up and down the system. Such mobility allowed them to feel that the hierarchy was informed by the function of providing people with challenging, growth-inspiring new jobs. Furthermore sannyasins at Medina believed that they were all equal in Bhagwan's eyes. Whatever external differences existed between them, they said, we are basically the same.

One factor needs to be emphasized in explaining why sannyasins at Rajneeshpuram, Medina, and presumably the other communes, did not experience their freedom being curtailed. They had learnt to look to their inner being to find liberty. They had also learnt that to surrender to external rules is a necessary condition for obtaining this freedom. Bhagwan says, 'I am showing you a way where there is no need for any structure inside. Consciousness can remain unstructured. That is the meaning of the word "freedom" '[6] In accord with this, sannyasins were prepared to accept whatever ways Bhagwan provided for them. They had an extremely strong tendency to interpret rules, directives, and U-turns as instruments of surrender, as devices for recognizing resistance in the form of beliefs or overactive egos. They felt that this kind of surrender would allow them to drop their ego-attachments, thereby allowing true meditation or liberation. Participant reports clearly show this to have been the case. Thus sannyasins whom we spoke to at the Medina felt they were on the path to freedom. They saw structure as a way of revealing the divine.

Another explanation of sannyasins' increasing obedience derives from their utter trust in Bhagwan. It is not simply that their love for him blinded them to the flaws of his path. More fundamentally, they have come to feel that he is an all-knowing, all-seeing, infallible Master, acting for the best of his sannyasins even when his actions seem mad. Madness in this sense is an ego-judgement. Trust for Bhagwan is not. So trust is followed. Hence the reaction to AIDS. When Bhagwan made his pronouncement in 1983 few in Britain were willing to accept that AIDS was as serious a problem as he said, or indeed as it has turned out to be. However, sannyasins responded with faith and gratitude:

> I have this man, this heaven-sent person, come to warn me about it. He is willing to give me stringent advice about surviving AIDS. It's like Noah's Ark. Can you imagine anything crazier than having to collect two of every animal? It's beyond one's comprehension, but you do as you are told because it's for a reason. If all this doesn't come to pass, if it's preposterous, then in some way it still serves me. It's a gamble worth taking. I'm quite willing to be seen as an idiot over this. Although it's hard, because obviously you want other people to respect the man you follow.
>
> (Chinmaya)

> As far as AIDS is concerned, I am just incredibly grateful I have a Master who is so practical.
>
> (Divya)

He gives us so much. For example, over this announcement on AIDS. I hadn't realized that it was as big as it is, and when I heard I was shocked. But I have completely accepted what he said. Whether I believe all the facts or not is irrelevant. It is not blind trust I feel for him. But he shows me the way. He is not going to do anything or say anything that will not give to me. I know that and I have total faith in his insight. The questions come up but they go away as well, and it doesn't matter that I don't always understand the reasons behind things.

(Pankaj)

We have been discussing some of the ways in which rules and commands have operated in the movement, as well as why sannyasins have gone along with increasing curtailment of what the outsider would see as their individual liberties. We have argued that sannyasins have accepted the change for a variety of reasons. For example, we have suggested that rules have been accepted because they are seen as techniques of transformation, as necessary to protect sannyasins from outside threats (eg. carriers of AIDS), and as necessary for the organization of daily life (recall Chinmaya's point that just as one needs a highway code, so one needs a code for living in a community).

There remains the possibility that sannyasins obey Bhagwan's dictates because they have become mindless automatons. Perhaps they have lost their ability to think for themselves, becoming orange-clad clones conditioned to follow Bhagwan's every move. After all, have not many been following a path which diverges very considerably from what initially attracted them? Is not the simplest explanation of why sannyasins relinquished their rule of freedom by allowing some of their members the freedom to rule that they have been indoctrinated?

Thinking of the situation at Rajneeshpuram, it appears that the goal of freedom has come to be secondary to faith in Bhagwan. It seems incontestable, particularly in the light of Bhagwan's 'concentration camp' pronouncement, that many sannyasins in the communes have abnegated their responsibilities: they have become too obedient, too attached to the system.

Our own impression is that sannyasins of the 'Sheela days' at Rajneeshpuram had indeed become too conditioned. Bhagwan would agree. What has happened is that the machine, which is after all how he describes the ego, had been allowed to reassert itself. Hence we find exactly the same kind of conditioning which develops in pretty well any strong community, whether it be the army, drug rehabilitation units, or even some schools. The question which remains to be answered is why Bhagwan allowed this to happen. For if Bhagwan is not an enlightened 'context setter', able to use rules to liberate his sannyasins, then human nature (being what it is) will lead to the proliferation of rules. Bhagwan can then reimplement 'freedom', as he appears to have done recently. But the net outcome of unenlightened context setting, if that is what it is, is that the movement is doomed to *impotent* oscillation between the extremes of obedience and freedom.

7

The Case of Bhagwan Shree Rajneesh: 'A good way of being'?

*I am the best showman in the whole
history of man. This is my circus, and
I enjoy it immensely.*

Bhagwan Shree Rajneesh

Arthur Koestler once wrote a book, *The Lotus and the Robot*, describing how he went to India, visited a number of gurus, and then passed judgement. Most of the gurus failed the tests which he set. Koestler was disillusioned. A great many others, visiting the same gurus, have been captivated. This shows how difficult it is to judge spiritual masters. They cannot be assessed as one might assess the record of an academic or a politician. They are working in ways which transcend our normal manner of making sense of and evaluating people. To assess them in terms of everyday values is to miss the point that, if they are authentic, their actions belong to another order of reality. To say, for example, that Jesus cannot be the Son of God because he allowed himself to be crucified is to ignore the possibility that the crucifixion illustrates the mysterious workings of the divine.

For reasons such as these many of those who study religion say that it is not their job to pass judgement on those whom they are studying. They are not even happy with the advice 'by his fruits shall ye know him'. There is always the possibility that apparently appalling fruits are actually working in a spiritually or religiously efficacious fashion. Most Christians do not cease to believe in their God when faced with apparently unjustifiable suffering.

But let us, for the moment, put Bhagwan in the dock. The case for the prosecution is that Bhagwan has shown himself to be unenlightened. He is to be judged a fraud. The case for the defence is that he is what he claims to be. In accordance with our view that 'spiritual' matters cannot be assessed by students of religions or academics, placing Bhagwan in the dock might appear inconsistent. However, it is interesting to see how some might want to judge Bhagwan. After all, not everyone will be happy with our claim that spiritual matters cannot be judged by methods appropriate for more down to earth matters. So let us see what the prosecution has to offer, and how the defence responds.

One of the main strategies for the prosecution is to argue that Bhagwan is simply a 'get rich quick' capitalist, using religion to motivate a poorly-paid workforce. Bhagwan says that he is unattached to money, yet he uses a fleet of Rolls Royces, not to mention an expensive speedboat and two jets. His sannyasins work to provide this, remaining content because they believe that they are progressing to enlightenment. To compound matters, Bhagwan is clearly a capitalist of the worst order, not concerned with helping those in need. During Poona days, impoverished Indians in the streets around the ashram were totally ignored.

A related strategy used by the prosecution is to claim that Bhagwan has indoctrinated his followers. Group therapies and formal meditations, the argument goes, have nothing to do with 'dropping the ego'. Talk of spiritual experience is mere justification for what is actually the binding of the ego to Bhagwan's desires. The closed environment of the communes, the establishment of new identities through taking sannyas, the induction of stress and emotional arousal, the attacks on previous 'ego-commitments', the emphasis on surrender: all are seen as techniques of mind-control. Bhagwan is held to generate trance states in which his sannyasins are susceptible to suggestion and open to his teaching.[1] To strengthen this line of attack, critics point out that techniques of transformation can easily lead to mental distress and illness. Writing in 1983, Floether claims:

> The local mental hospital in Poona still carries evidence of some of the damage done to sannyasins in therapies and workshops. Several spiritual seekers had to be admitted to this hospital prior to being sent back to their home countries. In Bombay, the West German Consulate alone handled fifty to sixty such cases each year.[2]

The prosecution sometimes uses a rather different tack. Instead of seeing the sannyasins as hardworking clones, followers are portrayed as exemplifying the narcissistic, hedonistic attributes of the 'Me' decade. Well-heeled Westerners have been attracted to a movement which allows them to indulge in their fantasies, whether sexual, aggressive, materialistic (remember the luxurious nature of the ashrams), or spiritual (the fashionable 'guru-trip'). On this account, sannyasins are like spoilt brats indulging in what has been frowned upon at home. Medina has been described as housing a 'bizarre "free-love" cult'. With 'Jaguars and Mercedes parked in the drive', with 'orgies' going on inside, the picture painted is of hedonism writ large. [3]

This leads to another line of attack, namely that the movement is morally reprehensible. It is not simply that it has been claimed that 'there is no such thing as sin for them'. [4] It has also been asserted that Bhagwan and his followers have been perfectly happy to work in immoral, deceitful ways to obtain their ends. It is claimed that girls from the Poona ashram were used to smuggle drugs into Europe. More recently, there is the episode of the 2,000 or so vagrants. Ostensively invited to Rajneeshpuram to be given a new chance in life, the extraordinary coincidence is that they arrived just at the time to swell numbers, votes being required to win a local election. After the election many of those tramps who wanted to leave were bussed to Portland and left to fend for themselves. [5]

The picture of Bhagwan as a machiavellian manipulator is further born out when one considers the nature of his teaching. Attending to this, the prosecution is able to make an additional accusation, namely that Bhagwan is simply a bad, unoriginal, incoherent guru. The teaching, it is alleged, is wracked with so many contradictions as to be unintelligible. On the one hand, he talks of emptiness, of getting rid of the mind, of renouncing all that is illusory. On the other, he talks of accepting all that is, of incorporating ego-functions, of encompassing the darkness as well as the light. Bhagwan has also been accused of being contradictory in more specific regards. In Poona days he insisted that he would never leave India. America was described as 'a place for the mentally sick'. On moving to the United States he came to talk of his new home as being 'the most liberal country in the world'. On returning to India he now speaks of America as being peopled by 'sub-human monsters'. Whereas he had seen Americans as being ready for spirituality he now claims that 'the whole world beyond India lives in a materialistic age. Eat, drink and be merry is their decision, which is hilarious, absurd.' [6]

On the basis of these and many other contradictions the prosecution can make a number of allegations. First, it can be claimed that Bhagwan is simply confused. Selecting themes from a great many religious masters (such as Jesus and Buddha) to give authority to his path he has failed to mesh the teachings together into a coherent picture. Second, the claim is made that Bhagwan continually tailors his message to suit his audience, telling his sannyasins what he wants them to hear. When it suits him he tells them that it is fine to be wealthy and unrestrained; but only when it suits him. Third, it is said that Bhagwan has either made mistakes about specific matters or has changed his opinion about them to try and retain some credibility in the face of changing circumstances. It would have been hard to exercise appeal in America had he persisted in describing Americans as mentally ill. It certainly looks as though the reason why Bhagwan makes one judgement at a particular time and the opposite at another is that he has been a victim of circumstances, including the fact that he himself has made mistaken judgements.

Criticisms of Bhagwan are legion. In passing we can also mention other points which might be raised by the prosecution. They could argue, for example, that Bhagwan has attracted rather weak, aimless people by presenting them with powerful baits, such as is provided by his role as a surrogate father.[7] Or they could point to Bhagwan's undoubted charisma, arguing that his sheer magnetism alone has attracted people. The argument goes that Bhagwan has carefully nurtured his charisma by appearing as a media guru, packaged in numerous books and videos, possessing a flair for publicity and in general exercising the allure of his sparkling black eyes, carefully wild beard, and captivatingly delicate movements. Not to speak of the famous Bhagwan 'sssss', the noise he makes after words such as 'release'.

The criticisms made so far are relatively unimportant: at least when compared with the crux of the prosecution's case. Recent events at Rajneeshpuram, it is claimed, show that Bhagwan is a fraud. He is too fallible to be enlightened. Indeed, he could be fallible to the point of being criminal.

An important factor is that Bhagwan's contradictoriness has been highlighted. His teaching appears to have been drastically revised. The man who had taught the value of total surrender now says, after Sheela's departure, 'I teach independence. Be sceptical'[8] The man who had declared 'I am the founder of the one and only religion'[9] now says 'for the first time in the history of mankind a religion [Rajneeshism] has died. I never wanted it to be born in the first place.'[10] The man who had once set himself apart as something different now teaches that he is an 'ordinary man', not a god.[11] (He has indeed recently danced with sannyasins on the disco floor.) The prosecution points out that there is strong circumstantial evidence that these changes are a machiavellian response to what has happened in Rajneeshpuram. A victim of circumstance, including those of his own making, Bhagwan has made the best of a bad job by changing his teaching in order to dissociate himself from the mess involved in Sheela's departure. Hounded by events outside his control he has bent to the wind by changing tack.

Nowhere is the contradictory and strategic nature of Bhagwan's behaviour more in evidence, the prosecution alleges, than in his attitudes to Sheela. In mid-1985 he said:

> Look at her. She is so beautiful. Do you think that anything more is needed? She can manage this whole commune. I have sharpened her like a sword. I have told her to go and cut off as many heads as she can. [12]

Within a short time, all had changed. It was Sheela who had been saying 'Believe, surrender. All these things [for example, the use of firearms] are coming from Bhagwan.' It is Sheela who is referred to as Hitler: 'The glad news—this commune is free from a fascist regime. Adolf Hitler has died again.' [13] The prosecution concludes that these contradictions show Bhagwan to be a bad judge of character. Another conclusion is that Bhagwan has had to contradict himself by acknowledging that he did not know what he was doing and so was getting things wrong, when, for example, he founded Rajneeshism.

Thus far we have only skirted what the prosecution can infer from recent events as Rajneeshpuram. Exploring this in greater detail, the most radical accusation that can be made is that Bhagwan was the mastermind of what has happened. On this interpretation Bhagwan created a concentration camp in order to extort dollars. This, broadly speaking, is in line with Sheela's accusations. If such was indeed the case it is difficult not to conclude that Bhagwan is a fraud. He has lied, for as we shall see he claims that he was unaware of the mess that was developing. He has been party to illegal activities, and so on.

Somewhat less radically, it can be claimed that Bhagwan knew about, but did not encourage, at least some of the activities that were occurring. This account has Sheela plotting behind the scenes. What he was aware of, though, was that Sheela was introducing an increasing number of rules, developing a hierarchical structure, and the like. If this indeed was the case, the prosecution can argue that his stature as an enlightened being is discredited. Amongst other things, his failure to arrest the development of the 'concentration camp' entails the fact that he is morally reprehensible. Surely an enlightened being would step in to prevent the destruction of his path. It hardly reflects well on his previously stated aims that he should consciously have allowed the 'concentration camp' to develop. Neither does it reflect well on his powers of discernment that the guru of anti-culture should support and praise Sheela as the harbinger of the developing organization.

The prosecution has another line of attack. They could explore the implications of Bhagwan's own 'defence', namely that he did not know either that Sheela was plotting behind his back *or* that the commune was developing into a concentration camp. Bhagwan has claimed, 'The people in power at Rajneeshpuram took advantage of my silence. Because I was not in contact with my sannyasins I was not aware what was being done to them.' In the same interview, which took place just after Sheela left and when he claimed that he had just found out about how his commune had been managed, he said, 'In silence I was unaware. Only yesterday I heard these things.' [14]

Cut off from much of the daily life of the commune, apparently in close contact with only three people, [15] possibly living in a 'blissed-out' state, Bhagwan was simply unaware of the way events were transpiring. The prosecution might well be happy to accept this 'defence'. After all, it is damning. 'Bhagwan the unaware' is a pretty poor guru. Perhaps he was so 'blissed-out' and isolated as to be unaware of developments, but surely this is not the way to fulfil his avowed intention of helping his sannyasins to enlightenment. Given his teachings, given his stated purpose of coming back to this world for a further lifetime in order to help his disciples, given his continual insistence on the ease with which the ego and its garbage can take hold, Bhagwan should surely have exercised greater and more responsible supervision. He certainly appears to be too blind and irresponsible for a guru who believes that the ego is the realm of 'condensed unawareness'. It certainly does not appear to be the mark of an enlightened being to pay so little attention, for example, to the significance of the guns which surrounded him on his daily excursions.

With several lines of attack, the prosecution appear to have Bhagwan cornered. Ignorance of what was going on reflects ill on his spiritual standing. So does knowledge. Thinking only of his accusations against Sheela, blame is justified if he had been ignorant of her more harmful activities (but is this ignorance justifiable?); blame is unjustified if he had knowledge of what she was doing (for

Police station, Crete, 1986.

surely it is wrong to blame her in order to explain away the mess if he already knew what she was doing). Bhagwan certainly seems to have a lot to answer for.

Attacked by a religious fanatic in 1980, buildings burnt in 1981, bombs in Oregon and, apparently, the threats posed by Sheela: perhaps the violence of the response is not surprising. But is there any real substance to the case against Bhagwan? Is he really a greedy, irresponsible, mistake-prone fraud doing his best to avoid being a victim of what he has either encouraged or allowed to happen?

A number of the accusations against Bhagwan can be dealt with easily. The most obvious strategy for the defence to adopt is to point out that a great many things which Bhagwan has said and done are to be found in other traditions. Here we are referring to traditions whose authenticity is not challenged. Zen masters are notorious for their confrontational and contradictory ways. Mystics the world over are contradictory, saying things akin to Bhagwan's 'flowers of emptiness'. [16] Meditations of an even more dynamic, sexually arousing and disquieting nature can be found in tantric traditions. (At least to the best of our knowledge Bhagwan has never told anyone to 'eat shit'.) Another widespread teaching is that it is perfectly in order to be little concerned with the problems of the world outside when effective change has to derive from transformation of the inner being. Indeed, closed monastic orders in the West are in general only focused on the world beyond. As for wealth, the Roman Catholic Church is hardly poor.

Together with this line of defence, specific accusations can be refuted on the basis of hard evidence. The accusation of hedonism certainly does not apply today, since commune members have to work twelve hours a day, seven days a week. The accusation that sannyasins are placed in suggestible states through practising formal meditations and being involved in group therapies does not apply because commune members do not practice any such techniques. Nor is there any solid evidence for the claims that drug-running and prostitution (which might well have taken place) were masterminded by Bhagwan. Nor, at the time of writing, has Sheela substantiated her allegations. Indeed it is Sheela who is currently in prison, awaiting trial on charges more or less identical to those initially levelled against her by her master.

Then there is the question of psychological casualties. No doubt group therapies and formal meditations sometimes trigger unwelcome states of mind, but then so do university examinations and business or military training. Indeed, many institutions, such as marriage, can have undesirable effects. The defence would ask for statistical evidence that Bhagwan's techniques of transformation have a higher incidence of casualty than other institutions which we accept. A related accusation is that Bhagwan attracts weak, emotionally disturbed people. Emotionally crippled people are hardly likely to have advanced in the world as so many sannyasins have done before (and after) taking sannyas. These appear as successful, stable citizens. Bhagwan certainly attracts some weak characters; but then, which institution does not?

So far so good. However, the defence is left with a number of more tricky issues. How is the defence to explain away Bhagwan's apparent mistakes (for example when he said in 1981 that if a new step was going to happen anywhere it would be in America)?[17] Or his apparent misjudgement of Sheela? What of the facts that he does not appear to have taken responsibility for his Buddhafield and that his attempt to combine freedom and structure has failed? Indeed, there are many things which are hard to square with Bhagwan's status as a spiritual leader.

The essence of any defence of Bhagwan is that he has allowed things to happen as they have done. *Everything* Bhagwan does or allows to happen can be seen as a technique of transformation. Bhagwan's teaching is not a systematic philosophy to be assessed in logical, conceptual, or moral terms. It arises out of the moment and is appropriate only in that moment. The truth is to be judged in terms of what is done. What is useful, and so true at one moment, can be discarded the next if it no longer serves to enlighten. As we saw in the first chapter, Bhagwan is concerned with 'being' not 'knowledge'. He is against facts, beliefs, and consistency: all must jockey for position behind the overriding imperative of appropriateness. That Bhagwan is not interested in uttering eternal truths but in using whatever is appropriate to reveal the truth within means that he cannot be criticized for contradicting himself. The many examples of Bhagwan's contradictions cannot be treated as literal statements. During the Poona days Bhagwan said much that set him apart from his sannyasins. He also stressed how much he had in common with them. The contradictory nature of his standing is resolved when one understands that his god-like claims are a technique of transformation:

I'm creating a fiction here. The fiction of the Master and the disciple, the fiction of the god and the devotee. It's a myth really. You can move through the myth to reach the truth. [18]

The argument is that Bhagwan is a 'context setter', consciously creating environments to benefit his sannyasins. Context setting explains the 'garbage' which appeared at Poona. He created an environment in which people could indulge in their ego-trips in order to rid themselves of their ego-attachments. As he put it:

The whole point of the environment is geared towards bringing the ego to light. Through continual buffeting of one will against another, finally and frequently the ego has to rear its head in protest—thereby exposing itself for all to see. But this is all part of the process. Only through a recognition and crystallization of the ego can it be dropped. [19]

He has also said, it will be recalled, 'Anything incomplete is carried by the mind forever and ever. Anything complete is dropped.' [20] The gist of this is that sannyasins must be allowed to become aware of and consciously live 'through' anything produced by their egos, especially 'garbage'. Those with a love of authority must be allowed to exercise this to the full. In Bharti's words, 'He'll give a power-hungry person more power, a greedy person more presents, an arrogant person more situations to feel superior.' [21]

Replying to a sannyasin who pointed out to him that many of his followers at Poona were engaging in power plays and the like, Bhagwan said, 'I'm perfectly aware of what goes on here. These are the situations I want to be created. They're my instruments.' [22] Unfortunately, the context-setting argument does not seem to work so well as a justification of recent events at Rajneeshpuram. As we have seen, Bhagwan claims that he was unaware of much that was going on—hardly the stance of a skilled context setter. Furthermore, Rajneeshpuram appears to have rarely provided the kind of setting which could 'foster spiritual growth by allowing individuals to be open to change'. [23] The commune itself contradicts Bhagwan's previously declared intention of establishing an environment 'in which no-one would function in a stereotyped established position'. [24] If Bhagwan is to be taken literally when he says that he was unaware of what was happening, he must have lost his grip on the environment. By default he allowed a situation to arise in which ego-attachment resulted in more and more mess rather than detachment. In the light of this, perhaps it might be argued that Bhagwan has become a new type of context setter. He withdrew from his sannyasins in order to give them the freedom to reveal fully and work through the machinations of the ego. Even though he must have known that egos would take control he let his sannyasins get on with it so that they could come to realize and dispense with still more of their 'trips'. He allowed them to see the consequences of their attachments, to become 'fixed'. He could then come back into the picture to pull the rug from under their feet, saying, in effect, 'Look, this is what happens when you get too attached to the periphery'. In such a fashion sannyasins can learn from the events at Rajneeshpuram. Bhagwan's purpose, one can argue, was to provide a demonstration of the powers of the ego. Sheela and her cohorts can be pointed to as an illustration of how the poisoning ego can corrupt the fairest vision.

The argument that Bhagwan has provided a lesson in the importance of his path might seem rather far-fetched. However, as we pointed out earlier, Bhagwan cannot be judged in the same way as someone who is not making spiritual claims. Bhagwan *could* be working in mysterious and enlightening ways. The argument that an ignorant 'blissed-out' guru is a pretty poor one ignores the fact that Bhagwan's withdrawal might have been appropriate. After all, Genesis says that Yahweh did nothing to stop Adam and Eve from exercising their freedom. The arguement that Bhagwan is too poor a judge of character to be enlightened might equally well be applied to Jesus' response to Judas: both might have been aware of their respective traitors, but neither did or said anvthing to prevent the treachery.

What all this adds up to is that Bhagwan's claims cannot be falsified. What he has done, or allowed to happen, need have no bearing on his stature as an enlightened being. Bhagwan is surely correct when he maintains that the mind is unable to fathom the workings of the mystical. Events at Rajneeshpuram certainly stretch his credibility. But a conclusive case against him cannot be made. The prosecution cannot prove that Bhagwan is unenlightened because he acts in an immoral and indulgent way. Conversely, the defence cannot establish that what appears immoral and indulgent is actually bound up with enlightenment.

Indefinite adjournment of the case is pronounced. However, it is not without significance to see how the sannyasins themselves have weathered the recent storms. As far as we can tell, the answer is, 'remarkably well'. The faith of most appears intact. Bhagwan has emerged unscathed. Growth still appears to be the order of the day. Says Veetdharm of the aftermath:

> It's dawning on us all that Bhagwan has opened yet another door for us, taking us to yet another level of freedom and responsibility. [25]

And, to close, the retrospective comments of the Editor of *The Rajneesh Times*:

> Bhagwan is the heart of this commune [Rajneeshpuram], the underlying current and inspiration for our being gathered anywhere. Some have been desperately in love with Him, desperately afraid of losing Him, and were willing to chase Him anywhere, even to Central Oregon.
> What we did here was basically impossible. We scraped together millions of dollars, slogged through the seasons of mud and dust, and worked so many hours that the days began to dissolve into one another. However, Bhagwan was not responsible for what we did. He had insisted endlessly that we are born alone, we live alone, and we die alone. WE are responsible for everything. It is a hard lesson, in this freezing season as we watch the government crouched and ready to pounce from a thousand directions. We watch in astonishment the continuing betrayal of former leaders like Swami Krishna Deva.

He concludes:

> The rest of us 'who didn't do anything wrong', are guilty of being too innocent. We watched and sometimes cooperated while Ma Anand Sheela and her fascist gang ran roughshod over our friends, us, and anyone else who got in their way.
> But just because we were often wrong in our attitude doesn't mean that the Oregon politicians and press were right. To varying degrees, for different reasons, we all misunderstood the nature of the experiment, the nature of the man who was among us. We all proved what Bhagwan said. We are asleep. So, whatever we see is dream, whatever we do is unconscious.
> There was real nourishment, love and ecstasy at Rajneeshpuram. Otherwise, no-one would have come and no-one would have stayed. Things which might have taken us lifetimes to get round to we experienced at supersonic speeds.
> Bhagwan is gone, but He is still in our hearts. I love Him more than ever, but less desperately. [26]

It appears that for sannyasins, those with most knowledge, in experience, of the path, the verdict is simple: events have been of transformative value. And if it has been of value to them, who are we as outsiders to ignore this in our considered response to Bhagwan's path? As anthropologists, we ourselves feel that participant testimonies are part of the ethnographic record which must be seriously attended to by those interested in exploring what is open to human experience.

Notes

Chapter 1

1 Vasant Joshi, *The Awakened One* (Harper & Row, 1982), p. 27.
2 The description of Bhagwan's enlightenment is taken from Joshi, *The Awakened One*, pp. 51–65.
3 Joshi, op. cit., p. 80.
4 Ibid., p. 88.
5 Rajneesh, *Meditation: The Art of Ecstasy* (Sheldon Press, 1980), p. 6.
6 Ram Chandra Prasad, *The Mystic of Feeling* (Motilal Banarsidass, 1978), p. 16.
7 Rajneesh, *The Discipline of Transcendence*, vol. 2 (Rajneesh Foundation, 1978), p. 107.
8 Joshi, op. cit., p. 119.
9 Ma Satya Bharti, *Death Comes Dancing* (Routledge & Kegan Paul, 1981), p. 117.
10 Bob Mullan, *Life as Laughter* (Routledge & Kegan Paul, 1983), p. 23.
11 Joshi, op. cit., p. 123.
12 Rajneesh, *The Secret of Secrets,* vol. 2 (Rajneesh Foundation, 1983), p. 137.
13 'Tratak' is 'fixed gazing or staring'. 'Kirtan' is an Indian devotional song involving repetitive chanting.
14 Joshi, op. cit., p. 119.
15 Ma Satya Bharti, op. cit., p. 72.
16 Joshi, op. cit., p. 135.

17 Rajneesh, *The Secret of Secrets*, vol. 2, p. 137.
18 *The European Buddhafield*, 17.4.81.
19 Circular to Rajneesh Centres worldwide.
20 *Rajneeshism* (Rajneesh Foundation, 1983), p. 11.
21 Ibid. p. 54.
22 *Rajneesh Times* (British Edition), 5.11.84.
23 Unless otherwise indicated, material for the rest of the chapter has been provided by the sannyasin Press Officer in the UK, other sannyasins and Reuters. See also *The Guardian* 18.9.85, 13.10.85.
24 *FAIR News*, 11.85.
25 Rajneesh, talking at a press conference in Oregon following Sheela's departure, 11.85.

Chapter 2

1 Rajneesh, *The True Sage* (The Rajneesh foundation, 1976), p. vii.
2 Ibid., p. 17.
3 Ibid., p. 126 – 7.
4 Ibid., p. 29.
5 Ibid., p. 142.
6 Sally Belfrage, *Flowers of Emptiness* (The Woman's Press, 1981), p. 203.
7 Rajneesh, *Neither This Nor That* (Sheldon Press, 1978), p. 135.
8 Ma Satya Bharti, *Death Comes Dancing* (Routledge and Kegan Paul, 1981), p. 11.
9 Ibid., p. 11.
10 Rajneesh, *The True Sage* (The Rajneesh Foundation, 1976), p. 142.
11 Sally Belfrage, op. cit., p. 29.
12 Ibid., p. 28.
13 Rajneesh, *Meditation: The Art of Ecstasy* (Sheldon Press, 1980), p. xi.
14 Rajneesh, *The True Sage*, p. 309.
15 Ma Satya Bharti, op. cit., p. 11.
16 Rajneesh, *The Secret of Secrets*, vol. 2 (Rajneesh Foundation, 1983), p. 344.
17 Ibid., p. 267.
18 *The Rajneesh Times*, 17.2.84.
19 Rajneesh, *The True Sage*, p. 85.
20 Ibid., p. 344.
21 Ibid., p. 221
22 Ibid., p. 299.

23 Rajneesh, *Meditation: The Art of Ecstasy*, p. 17.
24 Rajneesh, *The True Sage*, p. 297.
25 Rajneesh, *Meditation: The Art of Ecstasy*, p. xx.
26 Rajneesh, *The Divine Illness*, (1974), p. 42.
27 Rajneesh, *Meditation: The Art of Ecstasy*, p. 104.
28 Vasant Joshi, *The Awakened One* (Harper & Row 1982), p. 119.
29 Rajneesh, *Meditation: The Art of Ecstasy*, p. 108.
30 Ibid., p. 110.
31 Ibid., p. 42
32 Ibid., p. 166.
33 Rajneesh, *Tantra: The Supreme Understanding* (Sheldon Press, 1978) p. 47.
34 Rajneesh, *Meditation: The Art of Ecstasy*, p. 165.
35 Ibid.
36 Rajneesh, *Philosophia Perennis* (Rajneesh Foundation, 1981), p. 9.
37 Bob Mullan, *Life as Laughter* (Routledge and Kegan Paul, 1983), p. 47.
38 Rajneesh, *Meditation: The Art of Ecstasy*, p. 110.
39 Rajneesh, *Philosophia Perennis*, p. 10.
40 *Rajneeshpuram: An Oasis booklet* (Rajneesh Foundation, 1983), p. 4.
41 Ibid., p. 9.
42 Rajneesh, quoted from an interview with US Immigration in Portland, Oregon, 14. 10. 82.
43 *The Guardian*, 17.11.85.
44 *Rajneeshpuram: An Oasis booklet*, p. 23.
45 *Rajneeshism* (Rajneesh Foundation, 1983), p. 19.
46 Ibid.
47 *Rajneeshpuram: An Oasis booklet*, p. 23.
48 Rajneesh, interview with US Immigration, 14.10.82.
49 Rajneesh, *The True Sage*, p. 17 – 18.
50 Rajneesh, *Philosophia Perennis*, p. 29.
51 Ibid., p. 23.
52 Ibid.
53 Rajneesh, *The Divine Illness*, p. 42.

Chapter 3

1 Rajneesh, *Meditation: The Art of Ecstasy* (Sheldon Press, 1980), p. 28.

2 Ma Satya Bharti, *Death Comes Dancing* (Routledge & Kegan Paul, 1981) p. 11.
3 Rajneesh, *The Secret of Secrets*, vol. 2 (Rajneesh Foundation, 1983), p. 52.
4 Sally Belfrage, *Flowers of Emptiness* (The Woman's Press, 1981), p. 53.
5 Formerly Paul Lowe, founder of Quaesitor which had been the most successful growth centre in Britain.
6 Sally Belfrage, op. cit., p. 135.
7 Ma Satya Bharti, *The Ultimate Risk* (Wildwood House, 1980), p. 114.
8 Ibid., pp. 126–9.
9 A former sannyasin, *No Ego, No I* (Aarhus University Research Centre, Denmark, 1980), p. 16.
10 Ibid.
11 Ibid., p. 17.
12 Sally Belfrage, *Flowers of Emptiness*, p. 198.
13 Ma Satya Bharti, *The Ultimate Risk*, pp. 182–3.
14 This description of 'spiritual therapy' comes from an article written by Rajen in *The Rajneesh Times*, 7.2.84.
15 Ma Satya Bharti, *Death Comes Dancing*, p. 81.
16 Ibid.
17 Rajneesh, *The Divine Illness*, (1974), p. 42.
18 Ma Satya Bharti, *Death Comes Dancing*, p. 17.
19 Unused to being expressive, some people find catharsis difficult. They are told to play-act uncomfortable emotions, this generally leading to genuine emotional display.
20 Ma Satya Bharti, op. cit., p. 25.
21 Ibid.
22 Rajneesh, *Meditation: The Art of Ecstasy*, p. 17.
23 Ma Satya Bharti, op. cit., p. 86
24 Vasant Joshi, *The Awakened One* (Harper & Row, 1982), p. 127.
25 Ibid.
26 Grada Rajneesh, a Dutch rehabilitation clinic for addicts run by Veeresh, retains this characteristic.
27 Ma Satya Bharti, *Death Comes Dancing*, p. 11.
28 *The Rajneesh Times*, 7.2.84.
29 Ma Satya Bharti, op. cit., p. 11.
30 *Medina brochure*, February–May 1984, p. 15.
31 See Bharti, *Death Comes Dancing*, p. 134.
32 Ibid., p. 11.

33 Rajneesh, *Neither This Nor That* (Sheldon Press, 1978), p. 218.
34 Ma Satya Bharti, op. cit., p. 79.
35 Sally Belfrage, *Flowers of Emptiness*, p. 10.
36 Rajneesh, *Meditation: The Art of Ecstasy*, p. 23.
37 A former sannyasin, *No Ego, No I*, p. 17.
38 *Medina brochure*, February–May 1984, p. 15.

Chapter 4

1 Bob Mullan, *Life as Laughter* (Routledge and Kegan Paul, 1983), p. 51.
2 *Preliminary report on the survey of the people of Rajneeshpuram*, 14.8.83; Hagan, Latkin, Littman, Sundberg, Department of Psychology, University of Oregon, USA.
3 Judith Coney, *The Lancaster Sannyasins of Bhagwan Shree Rajneesh* (unpublished).
4 'From Russia with Love', art. in *The Buddhafield Rajneesh European Newsletter*, 12.81.
5 See Bharti, *Death Comes Dancing* (Routledge and Kegan Paul 1982), p. 82. Additional material is provided by the report of Hagan and associates on Rajneeshpuram (14.8.83). Over a quarter of residents there in 1983 had a background in psychology.
6 Rajneesh, *The Secret of Secrets,* vol. 2 (Rajneesh Foundation, 1983), p. 406.
7 *Rajneeshism* (Rajneesh Foundation, 1983), p. 35.
8 Bob Mullan, *Life as Laughter*, p. 82.
9 Simon Winchester, *The Sunday Times Magazine*, 7.84, p. 22.
10 This figure is the official estimate, provided by the Press Office at Medina. Mullan offers a figure of 350,000; Bhagwan 1 million (*Sunday Times* 15.12.85).
11 Rajneesh, *The Secret of Secrets*, vol. 2, p. 406.
12 Eckhart Floether, *Bhagwan Shree Rajneesh and his New Religious Movement in America* (Intervarsity Press, 1983) provides a hostile account.

Chapter 5

1 *Rajneeshpuram the Rainbow* (Rajneesh Foundation, 1983), p. 10.
2 Rajneesh, *The Secret of Secrets*, vol. 2 (Rajneesh Foundation, 1983), p. 39.
3 The following detail has been largely provided by the Press Office, Rajneeshpuram (1983).
4 *Rajneeshpuram an Oasis* (Rajneesh Foundation, 1983), p. 4.

5 Vasant Joshi, *The Awakened One* (Harper & Row, 1982), p. 7.
6 Ma Mary Catherine, *The Rajneesh Times*, 6.7.84.
7 *The Statesman Journal*, Salem, Oregon, 3.7.83.
8 Vasant Joshi, *The Awakened One*, p. 155.
9 Bob Mullan, *Life as Laughter* (Routledge and Kegan Paul, 1983), p. 118.
10 Ibid., p. 121.
11 Quoted in *The Rajneesh Times*, British Edition, 15.5.84.
12 Ibid.
13 *The Sunday Times*, 8.7.84.
14 *The Daily Mail*, 1.5.84.
15 *The Rajneesh Times*, British Edition, 15.5.84.
16 Ibid.
17 Ibid.
18 *The Los Angeles Herald Examiner* 20.9.83.
19 *Asiaweek*, 29.7.83.
20 *The Los Angeles Herald Examiner*, 20.9.83.
21 *Oregon Magazine*, 1.84.
22 Interview with one of the authors, 12.83.
23 *The Guardian*, 17.11.85.
24 *Oregon Magazine*, 8.83.

Chapter 6

1 Rajneesh, *The True Sage* (Rajneesh Foundation, 1976), p. 57.
2 Spoken by Bhagwan on 24 March 1981.
3 Rajneesh, *The True Sage*, p. 220−1.
4 Quoted from a press conference given after Sheela's departure, 11.85.
5 Rajneesh, *The True Sage*, p. 35.
6 Rajneesh, *The Secret of Secrets*, vol 2 (Rajneesh Foundation, 1983), p. 195.

Chapter 7

1 Joan Gomez, *Explanatory Note, Transmarginal Mental States and the Indian Sect of Bhagwan Shree Rajneesh*, FAIR Brief, 1982.
2 Eckart Floether, *Bhagwan Shree Rajneesh and his New Religious Movement in America* (Intervarsity Press, 1983).
3 *The Daily Mail*, 30.4.84.
4 Ibid.
5 *Newsweek*, 24.9.84.

6   *The Guardian* 15.11.85; *City Limits* 22, 8.11.85
7   See Bob Mullan, *Life as Laughter* (Routledge & Kegan Paul, 1983), p. 155.
8   Press Conference.
9   *Der Spiegal* 5.8.85.
10 *The Daily Telegraph*, 3.10.85.
11 *The Times*, 29.10.85.
12 *The Sunday Oregonian*, 21.7.85.
13 Press Conference.
14 Ibid.
15 Ibid.
16 Sally Belfrage, *Flowers of Emptiness* (The Women's Press, 1981), p. 1, and William Stace, *Mysticism and Philosophy* (Macmillan, 1960).
17 *Rajneeshpuram an Oasis* (Rajneesh Foundation, 1983), p. 7.
18 Ma Satya Bharti, *Death Comes Dancing* (Routledge & Kegan Paul, 1981), p. vii.
19 Rajneesh, *Beloved of My Heart* (Rajneesh Foundation, 1978), p. 77.
20 Rajneesh, *Neither This Nor That* (Sheldon Press, 1978), p. 218.
21 Ma Satya Bharti, *Death Comes Dancing* (Routledge & Kegan Paul, 1981), p. 76.
22 Ibid., p. 74.
23 *Rajneeshpuram the Rainbow* (Rajneesh Foundation, 1983), p. 13.
24 Vasant Joshi *The Awakened One* (Harper & Row, 1982), p. 145.
25 *The Rajneesh Times*, 29.11.85.
26 Ibid.

Index

In the same series . . .
MY SWEET LORD

The Hare Krishna Movement

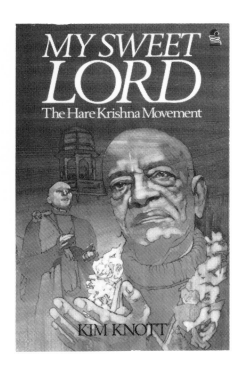

Despite—or perhaps because of—the attentions of pop stars such as George Harrison, the Hare Krishna movement is often widely dismissed as a new 'crank' or 'fad' religion. In fact its roots are as old as the roots of time. It uses the most famous Hindu incarnation of God—Krishna—as a point of attention from which self-realization and cosmic awareness can be found. The second volume in Aquarian's new Religious Movement series, this book offers a chance to understand, and practise, a religion which has brought personal, unselfish, satisfaction and peace of mind to many thousands of its devotees. **Kim Knott** here presents a well-balanced and easily read account of an authentic and living religion.

BLACK PARADISE

The Rastafarian Movement

'The Rastafarians, their faith and their aspirations, deserve more sympathy than they get from the British people.' Lord Scarman, 1981.

Most people are familiar with the 'dreadlocks' of Rastafarianism, but few are aware of the high ideology of this growing 'new' religion. **Peter B Clarke**, lecturer at the centre for New Religious movements, here presents an authoratative account of what must surely be one of the least understood, and most often maligned religions practised in Britain today. Describes in detail: the concept of God and Haile Selassie; Rasta languages, rituals and music; the role of women; use of ganja (marijuana) and the dreadlock hairstyle as a symbol of Rasta origins and aspirations.